❧ Cuba Libre ❧

Global History Series

KYLE LONGLEY, SERIES EDITOR
ARIZONA STATE UNIVERSITY

Paul J. Dosal
UNIVERSITY OF
SOUTH FLORIDA

Cuba Libre

A Brief History of Cuba

Harlan Davidson, Inc.
Wheeling, Illinois 60090-6000

Visit us on the World Wide Web at www.harlandavidson.com.

Library of Congress Cataloging-in-Publication Data

Dosal, Paul J. (Paul Jaime), 1960–
   Cuba libre : a brief history of Cuba / Paul J. Dosal.
      p. cm. — (The global history series)
   Includes bibliographical references and index.
   ISBN-13: 978-0-88295-246-8 (alk. paper)
   ISBN-10: 0-88295-246-3 (alk. paper)
   1. Cuba—History. I. Title. II. Series: Global history series (Wheeling, Ill.)
   F1776.D67 2006
   972.91—dc22
                                        2006002552

Cover photograph: A young Cuban holds a picture of José Martí during a
ceremony to mark his 150th birthday, January 28, 2003. *AP Photo/
Christobal Herrera.*
Cover design: Christopher Calvetti, c2it graphics

Manufactured in the United States of America
10 09 08 07 06 1 2 3 4 5 VP

To Lisa Dosal

🦋 Editor's Foreword 🦋

*F*ew countries have a richer, albeit more tumultuous, history than Cuba, a small island that played a large role in the history of the modern world. Cuba's strategic location at the entrance to the Caribbean and subsequent access to the vast resources of Mexico, the U.S. Gulf Coast, Central America, and the northern coasts of South America kept it in the eyes of the major world powers from the time Spain first colonized the island in the sixteenth century.

One of the last jewels to fall from the crown of the Spanish Empire, Cuba served for nearly four hundred years as a microcosm of the history of colonization and, eventually, the grueling process known as decolonization. The export-driven sugar economy, fueled largely by the massive infusion of enslaved Africans to replace a decimated pool of native laborers, created a unique society that blended different cultures from across the Atlantic world.

The nationalist wars of independence that wracked Cuba in the late nineteenth century, led by visionaries such as José Martí, provided revolutionary models for other countries in the non-industrialized world seeking to throw off the shackles of imperial control. These violent conflicts also marked the simultaneous decline of Spain and rise of the United States as a world power, a phenomenon that turned a local conflict into one with global dimensions. In the aftermath of a successful war of independence in 1899, Cuba would continue the long struggle to establish a viable nation state in the shadow of its more powerful northern neighbor, a struggle ultimately culminating in the 1950s with the rise of Fidel Castro, the man who established the first socialist state in the Western Hemisphere.

This phase of Cuba's revolution thrust it even more prominently onto the global stage. Castro's brand of nationalistic communism and defiant leadership soon inspired other peoples of the non-industrialized world. Those in rapidly decolonizing regions of Africa, the Middle East, and Southeast Asia looked on in amazement as Cuba, with the strong support of the Soviet Union, thumbed its nose at the major superpower only ninety miles from its shores. In the process, Cuba became a flashpoint in the Cold War, nearly leading the world into nuclear war during the Cuban Missile Crisis. Literally, the global political and economic structure hung in limbo during October 1962, as John F. Kennedy and Nikita Khrushchev, with a disgruntled Castro a very active participant, squared off over Cuban sovereignty.

Throughout the rest of the Cold War and into the twenty-first century, Cuba remained a prominent player in international relations, one far exceeding its comparative size and power. Cuban troops fought in wars in far-off places in Africa, and Castro remained a strongman in regional affairs, mentoring groups and individuals such as the Sandinistas in Nicaragua and Hugo Chávez in Venezuela. His profile stayed high and the Cuban experiment in socialist education and medical care earned the envy of other Latin American nations. The end of the Cold War and the cutting of Soviet subsidies certainly weakened Cuba, but it is still a vibrant nation, one perhaps on the brink of significant change with the death of Castro. Thus, it is important that all of us, as citizens of our respective nations and the global community, gain insight into Cuba's past as we prepare for its, and our own, future.

Cuba Libre: A Brief History of Cuba is the first volume in Harlan Davidson's Global History Series, a new line of books designed to provide readers with a concise and accessible survey of the subject nation as well as an understanding of its role in the global story. In the pages that follow, Paul Dosal delivers on that promise, for he has crafted a concise, fast-paced, and remarkably lucid overview of the complex history of Cuba, one that addresses the need for more comprehension of the subject and its interrelation to world history. Going beyond a description of major figures and events, Dr. Dosal weaves into the narrative major cultural trends—including cuisine, dance, and sports—as well as a consideration of Cuba's long relationships with major global powers such as Spain, Great Britain, Germany, the Soviet Union, and the United States.

It is my hope that those who teach courses in the history of Cuba, the Caribbean, Latin America, the Atlantic World, World History, and Comparative Global Studies will find this and future series volumes useful tools for teaching and that their students will enjoy and benefit from them as they ponder our world—past, present, and future.

Kyle Longley
Snell Family Dean's Distinguished
Professor of History
Arizona State University

❧ Contents ❧

🌿 Acknowledgments 🌿

*O*ne cannot tell the complete story of Cuba's complex and exciting history in less than two hundred pages. Therefore this book is, by design, more like "a sprint through a lavish and fascinating museum," to borrow the words of an anonymous reviewer. Clearly, almost every topic covered in this brief survey deserves fuller treatment and closer study by advanced students. Nevertheless, as Kyle Longley, editor of Harlan Davidson's new Global History Series, maintains, there is a need for a concise, accessible, and affordable survey of Cuban history, one useful as interesting supplemental reading in a variety of college-level courses. I am grateful to him for inviting me to write this history despite the inherent challenges it presented and for helping me at every stage of the process. Andrew J. Davidson, publisher and editor, also recognized the need for this book, and I appreciate his friendly advice and support.

Fortunately, the literature on Cuban history is rich and diverse. Historians, political scientists, economists, sociologists, musicologists, and others have studied aspects of the subject that by necessity receive only cursory treatment herein. Those works, however, have informed this study, and I encourage readers to browse through the bibliographical essay at the end of this book to find more extensive treatment on topics of interest.

I am a relative newcomer to the field of Cuban history. Having spent the early years of my professional career working on Central American history, I decided in 1993 to switch the geographical focus of my research and teaching to Cuba. I am a native of Tampa, Florida, a descendant of Cuban immigrants who settled in Ybor City in 1889. They supported the cause of Cuba Libre; one of them even fought in the Mambí army. I, former president of the *Círculo*

Cubano de Tampa, a mutual aid society founded in Tampa in 1902, have apparently inherited a belief in that cause.

Finally, I am thankful for the support and encouragement of my wife Lisa, a former Peace Corps volunteer in Honduras. She tolerated the long hours I put into this project with patience, even as the due date of our first child approached in January 2006. His birth is just a few days away as I write this. Lisa and I hope the he too will share our love of Latin American history and culture.

Paul J. Dosal
Tampa, Florida

❦ Preface ❦

On the evening of November 26, 1891, the Cuban cigar makers of Tampa, Florida, waited anxiously for José Martí to take the stage. Martí, a thirty-eight-year-old writer and political activist, had come from New York to organize this growing hotbed of Cuban patriots. Several thousand Cubans lived and worked in Ybor City, a company town founded on the outskirts of Tampa in 1886, but they planned to liberate their homeland from Spanish rule and return to a free Cuba. Rumors were spreading that Martí, an eloquent writer and inspiring speaker, would be the one to lead them back to their Promised Land. Nobody could describe a vision of *Cuba Libre* (Free Cuba) better than Martí, and the generals and politicians were already beginning to unite behind him. The independence movement had been stalled since 1878, when a ten-year war ended with an inconclusive truce and much bickering among the Cuban rebels. On this evening, the Cubans of Ybor City wanted to hear Martí tell them that the arguments would end and the fighting begin. They wanted action, and they expected this short, bald man to deliver it.

After brief introductions by local leaders, Martí rose to a thunderous applause and shouts of *¡Viva! ¡Viva Cuba Libre!* He folded his arms across his chest and appealed for silence: "For suffering Cuba, the first word." Not even a whisper could be heard as Martí continued slowly. "Cuba must be considered an altar for the offering of our lives, not a pedestal for lifting us above it." Too many Cuban leaders in the first war had put their personal ambitions and egos above the greater good of Cuba, and the bloody war had ended in failure. In the war to come, Martí demanded that everybody fight for a higher cause, and he had no doubt that these Cuban exiles knew exactly what he meant. "My breast swells with pride. At this moment I love my country even more

1

than before, and I now have an even greater faith in its serene and well-or-
dered future."

Martí depicted with exceptional elegance a vision of independent Cuba
that others only felt. The homeland of which they dreamed could be redeemed
only by creating a republic based on the highest standards of morality and
virtue. As Martí described it, the cause was more of a religious crusade than a
political movement. The first law of the new republic would be respect for the
full dignity of humankind. "Every true man must feel upon his own cheek the
slap upon any other man's cheek." If the republic were not founded on this
principle, Martí asserted that freedom would not be "worth one of our moth-
ers' tears or a single drop of our heroes' blood. . . . We are striving to liberate
Cubans and not to intimidate them," he explained.

By *Cuban* he meant every resident of the island, regardless of race, class,
or gender. There were Cubans of African origin in the audience, and the speaker
assured them that they too would assume full rights of citizenship in the new
Cuba. To the white Cubans who would deny black Cubans equal rights in the
new Republic, Martí said: "I know of black hands that are plunged further
into virtue than those of any white man I have ever met." Martí envisioned a
free society in which everyone would enjoy the same rights and privileges,
with no dominant group or class able to deny opportunities to others. There
also were women in the audience, and Martí expected them to join the struggle
to create an ideal republic, one free of discrimination. Finally, there were wealthy
Cubans in the audience; and Martí called on the "elegant young dandies" to
join a redemptive revolution that had already "made brothers of the heroic
first-born and the landless peasant, the master of men and his slaves."

Martí ended his political sermon with a call to arms. "Enough, enough
of mere words! . . . Now to form ranks. . . . Down there is our Cuba, smoth-
ered in the arms that crush and corrupt it for us. . . . There she is, calling to us.
We can hear her moan; she is being raped and mocked. . . . Our dearest mother
is being corrupted and torn limb from limb!" The crowd punctuated his sen-
tences with shouts and applause. "Let us rise up for the true republic. . . . Let
us rise up to give graves to the heroes. . . . Let us rise up so that some day our
children will have graves! And let us place around the star of our new flag this
formula of love triumphant: 'with all, and for the good of all.'"

Over the next four years, Cubans in the United States and Cuba organized an army of liberation. On February 24, 1895, this army of blacks and
whites, men and women, sugar planters and cane cutters, rose in rebellion.
Although Martí fell in one of the first skirmishes of the war for independence,
he had so ennobled the cause of Cuba Libre with a religious spirit and re-

demptive ideology that he is known reverently as the "Apostle of Cuban Liberty." The utopian republic built on a strong moral foundation was never conceived so beautifully as in the poetry of José Martí. He expressed a vision of Cuba that remains the ultimate ideal for Cubans of all political persuasions.

More than a century after the death of Martí, Cubans have yet to create the utopian republic. Cuba still suffers, condemned perhaps, to the predictable fate of a country burdened with an unattainable goal. Yet thousands of Cubans have fought and died for the cause. A million Cubans live in exile, and they, like the 11 million on the island, still believe in Cuba Libre and expect to see it in their lifetimes. On both sides of the Florida Straits, Cubans still intend to create the ideal republic, a country in which all citizens enjoy equal rights and promote the common good. In Havana and Santiago, Miami and Tampa, Cubans are still captivated by the promise of a just, egalitarian, and prosperous Cuba.

CHAPTER ONE

The Key to the New World
🔥 1492–1825 🔥

*E*uropeans first set foot on the largest island of the Antilles on October 28, 1492, when Christopher Columbus came ashore near Nipe Bay on the northeastern coast. Columbus described the island as "the most beautiful land that human eyes have ever seen." Indeed, with mountain ranges on both ends and vast fertile plains in the center, the island possesses a stunning and diverse natural beauty. Stretching 745 miles from west to east and covering more than 42,000 square miles, this "Pearl of the Antilles" guards the entrance to the Gulf of Mexico and the Caribbean Sea, a geographical fact that escaped the great explorer, who named the island Cuba, a corruption of the aboriginal name for it.

Neither the island nor its 60,000 inhabitants held much attraction for Columbus, who continued his journey to an island he christened Hispaniola, presently occupied by Haiti and the Dominican Republic. The indigenous people of Hispaniola received Columbus as friends, offering food, water, and shelter to the beleaguered Spaniards when they had to abandon one of their ships on Christmas day. With the assistance of the people on the northwestern shore of the island, Columbus founded Navidad, the first Spanish settlement in the Americas, near present-day Cap Haitien. Despite the friendly assistance he received, Columbus regarded the native people as primitive and uncivilized, valuable only as servants to his God and Spain. He therefore claimed the islands of the Caribbean on behalf of Queen Isabella and King Ferdinand, who were delighted at the exotic descriptions of the wealthy lands that Columbus had "discovered" for them.

Columbus sailed back the next year with 17 ships, 1,500 men, cannon, horses, and dogs. He had the authority to make war and the means to do it. When he discovered that Navidad had been burned to the ground and its

Spanish inhabitants killed, his voyage of exploration quickly became a military campaign. The conquest of the Americas began.

The native inhabitants of Hispaniola, mostly peaceable Taínos, resisted Spanish demands for their gold, labor, political allegiance, religious conversion, and women. The admiral himself led military campaigns against warriors who had never seen armored horsemen charge into battle with lances tilted at their chests. The island became a bloodbath, with Spanish swords and attack dogs leaving mangled corpses on the battlefields.

Hatuey, a Taíno chieftain who had fought the conquistadors in Hispaniola, fled the island and took refuge in eastern Cuba. There, he spread news of the atrocities committed by the Spaniards and their lust for gold. It would not be long before Spanish greed brought them to Cuba, he warned. As Hatuey feared, a Spanish expedition under the command of Diego Velásquez landed in Cuba in 1511, bringing the terror of the conquest with him. Hatuey organized the Taínos into an army of resistance in the mountains of eastern Cuba. Refusing to bow before the Spanish monarchs or their god, Hatuey and his force launched hit-and-run strikes against the superior Spanish forces. Hatuey fought courageously in defense of his homeland, but the crude weapons of his soldiers were no match for Spanish steel. The Spaniards eventually captured him and condemned him to be burned at the stake. As he awaited a gruesome death, a Franciscan friar offered him a place in heaven rather than an eternity in hell if he accepted the Christian god. Furthermore, if he converted, he would be strangled rather than burned to death, a measure of mercy that held little appeal to the native chief. "Will there be other Christians in heaven?" he asked. "Of course," the friar assured him. Hatuey told the good friar that he would rather go to hell, and the Christian flames sent him on his preferred way.

Hatuey died honorably in defense of his people, becoming the first martyr of Cuba, a relatively peaceful island until the arrival of the Spanish conquistadors. For generations, Cuban children have been taught to revere Hatuey as a symbol of resistance to foreign domination. The fact that he fought his oppressors in eastern Cuba, near the exact site where Carlos Manuel de Céspedes launched the Cuban war for independence in 1868, only adds to the mystique of the former. The Cuban patriots who followed in his footsteps consider Hatuey's heroic death a proper sacrifice in defense of Cuba Libre, even though they knew little of the actual cause for which he died. Over the next four hundred years, thousands of martyrs and patriots would fight and die on behalf of a Cuba conquered and colonized by Spain, the greatest military power of the sixteenth century.

CONQUEST AND COLONIZATION

From eastern Cuba the conquistadors marched westward, leaving death and destruction in their wake. The native inhabitants were ill prepared to resist the Spaniards. The Taínos, largest of the three native groups, were the latest arrivals and the most technologically advanced. Living in small villages and cultivating a variety of crops, including corn, yucca, and potatoes, the Taínos never possessed much of what the Spaniards seemed to value the most: gold and iron. They did, however, have their own forms of government and religion, and, as mentioned, they fought to defend their rights as an independent people. The other two indigenous groups, the Ciboney and the Guanahatabayes, were weaker than the Taínos, and they met the same gruesome fate. The Spaniards defeated the native armies, raped women, burned villages, and distributed Indian laborers to the conquistadors, who demanded work from their subjects in a system of tributary labor known as the *encomienda*. The physical abuse and exploitation suffered by the Indians in the encomienda system added to the rate of native mortality inflicted by disease and war. By 1544, the total native population of the island had been reduced to about 5,000. The Spanish conquest and colonization nearly eradicated an indigenous civilization, initiating a tragic cycle of racial and ethnic conflict that more than three centuries later Martí stood determined to eliminate.

The Spanish colonists initially founded seven settlements scattered across Cuba: Baracoa, Santiago, Bayamo, Puerto Príncipe, Sancti Spiritus, Trinidad, and Havana. In 1544, only 660 Spaniards lived in Cuba, and there were probably more pigs and cattle than humans on the entire island. Grazing in the abundant grasslands, the animals adapted to their new environment, devoured the crops of the Indians, and multiplied rapidly, carrying out a biological conquest of native animal and plant species that complemented the Spanish military campaigns. Over the decades, the herds of wild animals were a primary source of food for a few thousand Spanish colonists and the treasure fleets that called regularly at the island's ports.

Cuba simply did not have the rich deposits of gold and silver found in Mexico and Peru, so the Spanish quickly lost interest in colonizing the island. Instead, the Spaniards valued the island for its strategic location and near-perfect natural harbors, particularly Santiago and Havana. After 1553, when Spain ordered the governor to transfer his residence from Santiago to Havana, Havana began to emerge as the political, religious, military, and commercial center of the island. With a narrow channel leading into an expansive inner harbor, Havana was well positioned to defend Spanish shipping through the

Yucatan Channel and the Florida Straits, through which the treasures of Mexico and Peru passed to Spain.

The French, English, and Dutch, no less lustful for gold than their Spanish counterparts, rejected Spain's exclusive claims to American treasure and preyed on the Spanish ships and ports that possessed it. The first great theft of treasure destined for Spain came in 1522, when French privateers captured three ships, two of them bearing gold and silver from Mexico. When the French king received this unexpected prize, he exclaimed: "The Emperor [of Spain] can carry on the war against me by means of the riches he draws from the West Indies alone!"

Spain's rivals, fearing that American gold and silver would so enrich the King of Spain that they would lose power in Europe, knew that they had to attack Spanish wealth at its source: the Americas. By the mid-sixteenth century, the Caribbean had become a battleground for European superpowers. The Europeans valued Cuba and the Caribbean region not for the people or the resources in it, but primarily for the treasure that passed through it. The Caribbean lands, according to historian Eric Williams, became a "pawn of European power politics, the cockpit of Europe, the arena of Europe's wars hot and cold." Cuba, guarding the entrance to the Americas, has been at the center of European rivalries since Velásquez conquered it.

The French struck first. In 1555 Jacques Sores laid siege to Havana, which was defended by less than fifty men, women, and children. They barricaded themselves in a crude wooden fort adjacent to the harbor and fought off their attackers, but they could not hold out for long. Sores captured the fort, killed most of the defenders, and burned the city to the ground after the inhabitants offered a ransom of only a thousand pesos. The Spanish king, fearing a repetition of this tragedy, ordered the construction of a stronger fort to defend the city and the entrance to the harbor. This fort, Castillo de la Real Fuerza, possessed enough firepower to deter the most feared of all Caribbean treasure hunters, the English privateer Francis Drake, who appeared off the coast of Havana in 1585 with fourteen ships. Drake lingered offshore for a few days to study the fortifications of the city, but after firing a few shots their way, he moved on to other, more vulnerable prey.

The threat of foreign predators compelled the Spanish to fortify their Caribbean ports and develop a powerful navy. By the middle of the sixteenth century, the Spanish had established a convoy system to protect the annual shipments of gold and silver from the Americas. Two convoys set sail from southern Spain every year, one destined for Mexico and the other for Panama. After loading the gold and silver of Mexico and Peru, the two fleets assembled in Havana, from which Spanish warships would escort the king's treasure back to Spain. To protect the fleets and their treasures while in Havana, the Spanish built forts on each side of the narrow channel leading into the harbor. On the eastern cliffs rose Castillo de los Tres Santos Reyes Magos del Morro, commonly known as El Morro. On the western side of the channel sat a smaller fort, Castillo de la Punta. At night, Havana's defenders secured an iron chain between the two fortresses, creating an impenetrable barrier further protected by mighty cannons above it.

When the treasure fleets arrived in Havana, sailors, soldiers, merchants, and crewmen descended on the port city, its population already swelled to 10,000 by the carpenters, stonemasons, and slaves who worked on the city's fortifications. The fleets sometimes waited in Havana for weeks at a time, leaving idle crewmen with money to spend looking for food, lodging, and entertainment. Bars, brothels, and gambling dens proliferated, as did the crimes associated with them. Havana acquired a reputation as a sleazy, wide-open town, where visitors indulged their many passions and vices. By 1600 Havana was clearly the dominant city in an island colony of only 20,000 souls.

INTERNATIONAL RIVALRY IN THE CARIBBEAN

The residents of the island still lived in constant fear of an attack by foreign raiders. No city in Cuba, no ship that sailed around it or anchored in its harbors, was safe. French, English, and Dutch privateers regularly hunted for Spanish treasure and colonists in the small towns of eastern Cuba. The world beyond Havana was a deadly place, and the Cuban colonists developed a hatred of the foreigners who preyed on them. The greatest theft of Spanish treasure occurred in 1628, when Dutch commander Piet Heyn captured the entire Mexican treasure fleet. The Dutch heist yielded the greatest plunder ever taken by any Spanish rival: more than 177,000 pounds of silver and 135 pounds of gold. In the aftermath of Piet Heyn's theft, one colonist begged for revenge: "Who can hear of this and not seize high heaven itself in angry hands? Who at the risk of a thousand lives, if he had them, would not avenge so grievous an affront?"

Not even Havana, with is formidable fortifications, was completely secure. The completion of the Morro and Punta fortresses by 1630 offered more protection to Havana than any other city. If it was a city of sin, it was also a city of raw Spanish power. Havana's excellent natural harbor, guarded by seemingly impregnable fortresses, rendered it the strategic center of the Spanish empire in the Americas. By royal decree of 1634, Havana was officially declared the "Key to the New World and Bulwark of the West Indies."

Havana may have been the key to the Spanish Empire, but because Cuba lacked the great mineral resources of Mexico and Peru, the island's significance continued to rest on its strategic location. What little economic activity thrived there during the sixteenth and seventeenth centuries resulted from the demand stimulated by the forts and the fleets. This economy was centered in and around Havana, which grew in response to Spain's military and commercial needs. The economic stimulus provided by the visiting fleets spread into the central part of the island, where livestock grazed freely on the abundant savannas. From the plains came dried meat and hides for export.

The most prized commodity of early Cuba was tobacco. The native inhabitants of the island were smoking this noxious weed when Columbus arrived in 1492, and the Europeans quickly acquired a taste for it. As a taste for tobacco quickly developed into a habit, demand for tobacco soared in Europe and Cuban colonists responded, cultivating tobacco on small farms throughout the island by the early seventeenth century. Profits were high enough to attract the interests of both the Spanish crown, which wanted tax revenue, and smugglers, who wanted profits. Tobacco, relatively easy and cheap to cultivate, was a perfect item for the contraband trade; smugglers needed only a limited space to store the cargo, and it yielded a high profit. Colonists throughout the island engaged in an illicit trade with whatever English, French, or Dutch merchants called at their ports, defying one of the many commercial restrictions imposed on them by Spain. By the early 1700s, tobacco was Cuba's most important export.

Spain applied classic mercantilist economic policies to its American colonies, hoping to accumulate wealth in the form of gold and silver bullion by monopolizing all trade to and from its American possessions. In theory, Cuban commerce was reserved exclusively for Spanish merchants. Spanish law required the colonists to export their mineral and agricultural commodities to Spain and import all of their manufactured products from Spain. From Havana went gold and silver; to Havana went Spanish wines, wheat, equipment and clothes. Mercantilist theory clashed with economic reality, however, for Spain lacked the resources to meet all Cuban demands. To make up for frequent shortages, the colonists traded with any merchants who brought the commodities they needed. The colonists, particularly those in eastern Cuba, could not have survived long exclusively on the merchandise brought by the annual Spanish fleets. It was both necessary and easy for the colonists to defy royal regulations and trade illegally with Spain's enemies. By the beginning of the eighteenth century, a large percentage of Cuban commerce was conducted illegally.

The development of a flourishing contraband trade in Cuba brewed a political conflict between the colonists and the crown. The highest Spanish authority on the island was the captain-general, nominally subordinate to the viceroy in Mexico, and he was responsible for enforcing policies designed to defend and promote the interests of the Spanish empire, not Cuba. In practice, being several weeks away from Mexico and at least six weeks away from Spain, the captain-general enjoyed enough political autonomy to forge working relationships with representatives of the Cuban aristocracy. The residents of Cuba wanted to defend themselves against foreign attacks, an objective shared by the captain-general, but they also wanted to obtain goods at the cheapest prices, a practice prohibited by Spanish law. The *Creoles*, persons of Spanish descent born on the island, increasingly favored policies designed to protect and promote the economic development of Cuba. The *Peninsulars*, Spanish-born residents who occupied prominent positions in the state, church, and military, had to defend Spain's monopolistic policies. Cuban Creoles saw no reason why they should not trade with foreign merchants, while the Peninsulars, most notably the captains-general, found it increasingly difficult to enforce royal regulations, especially when economic necessity compelled them to tolerate an illicit trade.

Despite the relative poverty of colonial Cuba, foreign powers still envied Spain's possession of this strategic island. The English sacked and looted Santiago again in 1662, stirring Spanish fears of a renewed English assault on the key to their empire. In 1655, Oliver Cromwell, "Lord Protector of Great Britain," dispatched a large military expedition to deprive Spain of at least a small portion of its Caribbean holdings. The fleet appeared off Havana and surveyed the city defenses. Not wanting to test the mettle of the three garrisons, the English then invaded and took possession of the most poorly defended Spanish possession, Jamaica.

From bases in Jamaica and elsewhere came yet another threat to the Spanish colonists: the buccaneers, an international band of adventurers who plundered Spanish ships and towns in the late seventeenth century. The most famous buccaneer, a Welshman named Henry Morgan who sacked Panama in 1671, butchered and tortured the colonists in eastern Cuba. The depredations of Morgan, like those of the privateers before him, sapped the Spanish of wealth and men, contributing to the decline of Spain at a time of rising English and French power in the Caribbean and around the world.

By 1700, Spain was clearly a second-rate power, its armies and navies depleted by two centuries of conflict, its gold and silver nearly exhausted. The death of Charles II, the last Spanish Hapsburg king, prompted a dynastic struggle in Europe that brought Spain into a war against England as an ally of France. The war, known as the War of the Spanish Succession, ended with a Bourbon king sitting on the throne of Spain, with a family compact sealing Spain's close ties to France. For the rest of the eighteenth century, the Bourbon kings of Spain, supported and encouraged by the more robust French crown, attempted to revive the stagnant economies of the American colonies, with the legal and illegal support of the British.

THE BRITISH OCCUPATION OF HAVANA

The War of the Spanish Succession concluded with the Treaty of Utrecht (1713), which gave the British merchants of the South Sea Company the exclusive right to supply slaves to the Americas. This concession, known as an *asiento*, also granted the company the right to send one annual shipload of merchandise to the Portobelo fair in Panama. The British took full advantage of the treaty to increase their legal and illegal trade throughout the Spanish colonies. The slave ships calling on Cuban ports also brought tons of contraband merchandise, to the delight of the Cuban colonists. Spanish officials were easily persuaded to ignore troublesome rules for cash or simply because the Cubans needed the English goods. Contraband trade, particularly in tobacco, continued to increase as a result.

The Spanish crown attempted to profit from the growth of this valuable commodity. In 1717 it established a monopoly on the cultivation and production of tobacco. The company, known as the *Factoría de Tabacos*, became the exclusive purchaser of all tobacco produced in Cuba, at prices that it fixed. Now, all Cuban tobacco growers could sell only to the Factoría de Tabacos, which was not obligated to purchase all the tobacco grown in Cuba, just the amount it wanted. Moreover, this royal monopoly actually attempted to discourage the processing of tobacco. The Cubans were not even supposed to roll cigars; instead, they were supposed to export the tobacco leaf to Spain to be rolled there.

Clearly, the economic policies and objectives of far-off Spain simply did not reflect the realities and interests of the Cuban colonists. In one of the first serious challenges to Spanish authority since Hatuey, tobacco growers in Cuba, known as *vegueros*, defended their interests with arms in hand. In August 1717, five hundred vegueros marched on Havana to protest the tobacco monopoly.

The Spanish crown bowed to this show of force, removing the governor and temporarily suspending the tobacco monopoly, but Spain was in no mood to compromise. The crown reinforced the Havana garrisons, anticipating further resistance to imperial policy. The factory resumed operations in 1720 and the vegueros rebelled again. This time, however, the Spanish military pursued the rebels, dispersing them farther west into the region known as *Pinar del Rio*, where they ironically discovered the ideal lands for the cultivation of tobacco.

The application of Bourbon economic policies to Cuba ended an era in which Cuba had benefited from royal neglect. The success of the tobacco monopoly encouraged the Spanish government to tighten its control over all Cuban commerce. By the establishment of the *Real Compañia de Comercio* in 1740, the crown aimed at nothing less than a complete monopoly over all of Cuba's foreign trade. This company, with the exclusive rights to trade all products between Cuba and Spain, exported Cuban tobacco, sugar, and hides and imported Spanish flour, wine, and foodstuffs. The company yielded excellent returns for its investors, but it did little to promote the development and diversification of the Cuban economy.

The royal monopolies, however, could not completely control Cuban trade. And neither they nor the Spanish navy could possibly prevent the Cubans from engaging in illicit trade. As mentioned, the colonists had to trade illegally with the British because Spanish goods were too expensive and too scarce. Moreover, the British paid good money for tobacco, so contraband trade between Cuba and Great Britain increased in the eighteenth century, despite Spanish efforts to suppress it. By some estimates, Cubans sold nearly 75 percent of their entire tobacco crop to English merchants illegally.

As the rift between colony and crown, Creole and Peninsular, widened, Spain fell into the first of several ruinous late-eighteenth-century wars. Spain watched the Seven Years War (1755–63) from the sidelines until the French pressured the Spanish to join an ultimately disastrous war against England in January 1762. Once Spain entered the conflict, its American colonies became primary targets for the British, who had already turned Jamaica and Barbados into productive sugar colonies while the Spanish Caribbean islands languished. Now Great Britain eyed nothing less than the key to the Americas: Havana.

The British dispatched a fleet of 54 ships and 4,000 troops under the command of George Keppel, Lord of Albemarle. The fleet appeared offshore of Havana in early June 1762. Lord Albemarle surveyed the fortifications of Havana, a city of nearly 40,000 residents defended by 15,000 soldiers, and concluded that any attempt to penetrate directly into Havana harbor would be futile. He therefore decided to attack Havana overland from behind it. It was a good decision. Cabaña hill, on the eastern banks of the channel, commanded the heights over El Morro and Havana but was not fortified. Lord Albemarle landed nearly 4,000 troops east of Havana at Cojimar, took the garrison there, marched on to Guanabacoa, and took Cabaña hill without much of a fight on June 11. Then British troops took up positions south and west of the city, completing the encirclement of Havana.

On July 1, the British began a ferocious bombardment of El Morro. The impregnable fortress lived up to its reputation, for the cannonballs hardly dented its thick walls. At this point the Spanish realized that if they could withstand the assaults and survive on their rations, disease might kill more British troops than their guns, so the Spanish resolved to hold out as long as possible. Finally, the British detonated mines under the walls of El Morro on July 30, 1762, opening holes big enough for British infantrymen to storm through them. After an hour of bloody, hand-to-hand combat, the British marines took El Morro and then threatened to pound Havana into dust. On August 13, the Spanish surrendered the Key to the Americas with merchandise valued at £3 million in its warehouses.

Cuba would never again be the same. Although the British occupied Havana for only eleven months, they awoke Cuba from its colonial slumber. The British abolished all the onerous Spanish taxes and opened Havana to free trade with Great Britain and its colonies. Now British and North American merchants poured into the harbor. More than seven hundred merchant vessels called on Havana during the period of British occupation, more than all the traders that had visited it in the previous decade. The British brought in capital, textiles, and slaves in unprecedented numbers. In less than a year, they brought in as many as 10,000 slaves, ten times the number of slaves traded by the Spaniards in any previous year.

By the Treaty of Paris (1763), the British withdrew from Cuba in exchange for Spanish Florida. Cuban Creoles, seeing the commercial benefits of British occupation, had offered little resistance to their foreign rulers. Many prominent Creoles collaborated with the British, including Sebastian de Peñalver and Gonzalo Recio de Oquendo, both of whom served as deputies to Albemarle. They and other Creoles recognized that the Spanish policies had obstructed Cuba's economic development, while the British brought in merchandise, capital, and slaves that Cuban businesspeople needed to develop their economy. Like their counterparts in Britain's North American mainland colonies, the immorality of slavery meant less to Cuban planters than the high profits they could make by using enslaved African laborers on sugar plantations.

Sugar had been produced on a small scale in Cuba since the early sixteenth century, but Cuban production lagged far behind that of the British and English plantations in Haiti, Jamaica, and Barbados. There, Spain's rivals had developed viable colonies out of resource-poor islands by exploiting and brutalizing African slaves. The path to prosperity thus highlighted by the slave masters in Great Britain and France, Cuban planters followed suit. In the 1750s, Cuba exported an average of 300 tons of sugar per year. After the British occupation, sugar exports surged to 2,000 tons per year in the 1760s and to more than 10,000 tons per year in the 1770s. Cuban production rose steadily thereafter, converting Cuba into a Caribbean sugar bowl that would equal and ultimately surpass Haiti and Jamaica in volume produced.

This sugar boom came at a high price in African lives. Between 1763 and 1789, Cuban planters purchased as many as 70,000 African slaves, few of whom would live more than a decade on a sugar plantation. Of the 272,000 inhabitants of Cuba in 1791, nearly 65,000 were African slaves. Cuban demand for African slaves was apparently insatiable. The crown yielded to Cuban pressure and lifted all restrictions on the importation of slaves in 1791. The number of African slaves increased dramatically thereafter, as did the production of sugar.

The Spanish attempted to channel the profits of this slave-based economic boom into its treasury by implementing a series of reforms in Cuba and throughout the colonies to boost commerce and production. In 1778, King Carlos III broke the commercial monopoly previously held by Seville, opening all Spanish ports to trade with twenty-four ports in Spanish America. The crown maintained the prohibition of trade between its colonies and all non-Spanish merchants, but the colonists continued to trade illegally with Spain's rivals. Most Spanish American trade, including that of Cuba, was carried on with British, French, and other Europeans. Spain had already lost control of its colonies.

One beneficiary of the boom in Cuban trade, legal and illegal, was the young United States. North American merchants had called on Havana during the British occupation and established a commercial relationship that grew stronger with each passing year. The merchants of New England prospered from a triangular trade, purchasing slaves in Africa, selling them in Cuba, and carrying Cuban sugar molasses back to Boston. In 1792, due to a war between Spain and France, the king of Spain opened Cuban ports to neutral and allied shipping, an allowance that further stimulated the growing trade between the United States and Cuba.

The Cuban Creoles welcomed the late-eighteenth-century economic boom, regardless of its origins in brutal slave labor. The British occupation had opened their eyes to the potential of the sugar industry and trade with England and the United States. To keep the Creole planters happy and loyal, the Spanish crown gave the Cuban aristocrats greater representation in Spain and more titles in the military and militia. Havana's growing aristocracy, its wealth and ambitions tied to sugar and slaves, gained greater access to the corridors of power than any other Creoles in Spanish America. Cubans gained high ranks in the regular Spanish army and commanded the Cuban militia, on which the depleted Spanish defenses now depended. The captain-general could not govern effectively or defend the island without Cuban assistance. The Cuban planters, tasting power and prosperity under the late Bourbon kings, were growing more loyal to the Spanish at the same time that other Spanish American Creoles were beginning to realize that only independence would bring them power and prosperity.

THE EMERGENCE OF CUBAN NATIONALISM

At the same time, Cuban Creoles were developing a consciousness of themselves as Cubans, a people separated from the mother country by more than just an ocean. In 1791, the Spanish crown authorized a group of planters led by Francisco de Arango to organize the *Sociedad Económica de Amigos del País* (Economic Society of Friends of the Country). Chartered by the government to promote economic development, education, and the diffusion of technology and information, the society reflected and promoted the growing power of the Creoles. Within four years, the Economic Society had 163 members. This institution, with chapters throughout Spanish America, provided a forum for the Creoles to air their grievances and promote their political and economic causes. Cuban Creoles no longer considered themselves Spanish colonists; they were becoming Cubans.

Separation from Spain, however, carried risks, including death. Treason was a capital offense, and the Spaniards had never shown any reservations about executing rebels. Furthermore, the presence in Cuba of Spanish army troops offered security in a society made increasingly insecure by the inhumane treatment of African slaves on the plantations. Economic success, hinging on slave labor, depended in turn on the use of force to discipline the workers and crush their rebellions, and 65,000 Africans could not be held in bondage without the application of raw, brute force. If the Creoles drove the Spanish governor out of Cuba, he would take his army with him, leaving the planters to face the inevitable slave rebellions on their own.

Creole nationalism grew in the shadow of the Haitian revolution, a bloody race war that haunted Cuban planters for generations. In 1791, Haiti's 500,000

Spanish America circa 1800

0   500   1000 Kilometers
0   500   1000 Miles

slaves rose against their oppressors to liberate themselves and their country. Led by Toussaint L'Ouverture (1743–1803), a former slave, the African slaves turned soldiers fought French, British, and Spanish armies for the next thirteen years, abolishing slavery and destroying the plantation economy in the process. Haitian sugar exports dropped from 70,000 tons in 1791 to 25,000 in 1802 and to a mere 2,000 pounds in 1825. The Haitian revolutionaries destroyed more than 180 sugar plantations and 900 coffee plantations. They tortured, dismembered, and burned their former oppressors, killing more than 2,000 French planters and putting thousands more to flight. Haiti emerged as an independent black republic in 1804, the only large Caribbean island without a plantation system or a white planter class.

To the Cuban planters, the Haitian revolution served as a terrifying example of what could happen in the absence of a European power. Many of the French planters fled to the safety of Cuba, bringing tales of horror along with their capital and technology. The influx of the French sugar aristocracy further boosted the sugar industry and strengthened the conservative instincts of the Cuban planters. The growing nationalism of the Creoles, meanwhile, was tempered by the realization that any move toward independence might expose them to a Haitian-style revolution. Despite their dissatisfaction with Spanish economic policies, they knew that the Spanish army protected their lives and properties.

But the Creoles were just beginning to realize the nature of their political dilemma. While they had already begun to articulate a sense of separateness, they also fought Cubans of African origin over the meaning of independence. To many Creoles, the concept meant nothing more than separation from Spain. To the African-born residents of the island, both free and enslaved, independence could only mean personal freedom. In 1795, Nicolás Morales, a freed African and the son of a slave, conspired to launch a revolutionary war in the Haitian tradition. He intended to abolish slavery and distribute lands to former slaves, inaugurating an agrarian revolution that would have targeted whites and their properties throughout the island. The Spanish authorities crushed this rebellion, as they did the subsequent slave revolts of 1811, 1812, 1825, 1830, 1837, 1840, and 1843. Clearly, the Africans, although repeatedly foiled in rebellion, did not accept their enslavement without a fight, and the planters remained dependent on the presence of the Spanish army.

The recurrence of the slave rebellions revealed a deep schism in Cuban society that the planters could ignore only at their peril. The Africans clearly did not share the power or the prosperity that the Creoles were beginning to taste, and their understanding of a free and just Cuba did not coincide with that of the Creoles. To the extent that the planters wanted a free Cuba, it would be free for them only, not their African slaves. They preferred to work within the Spanish Empire rather than fight against it, and they saw abso-

lutely nothing to be gained by freeing their slaves for any political or economic purposes. Any alliance between Creoles and African slaves for the good
of Cuba Libre was simply inconceivable at this time.

The African slaves on the island had also demonstrated a willingness to
fight for their own liberation, but they did not belong in the Cuba of which
the Creoles conceived. The newfound prosperity of the Creoles depended on
slave labor. Great Britain, the world's greatest slave trading power, had converted to the abolitionist cause, but the Creoles were just starting to profit
from it. In 1808, Britain and the United States abolished the Atlantic slave
trade. Spain succumbed to British pressure as well, agreeing to end its trade in
slaves by 1820. But, with Cuban plantations still dependent on slave labor,
Africans continued to arrive in Cuba in shackles, as if no treaties had ever been
signed.

Spain's submission to British pressure reflected a sad political reality for
the Peninsulars, who still governed the island: the Spanish Empire was either
dying or already dead. Rebellions had broken out on mainland Spanish America
following the French occupation of Spain in 1808. Within a few years, Argentina, Paraguay, and Uruguay had gained de facto independence from Spain,
while patriots in Mexico, Colombia, and Venezuela fell short in their campaigns to liberate their parts of Latin America. The patriotic armies being
organized by Simón Bolívar (1783–1830), a Venezuelan Creole, and José de
San Martín (1778–1850), an Argentine Creole, represented a serious threat to
Spanish rule in Cuba. If and when they liberated Spanish South America, they
might attack Cuba, for they wanted to expel Spain from the entire Western
Hemisphere. Independence, it seemed, might come to Cuba whether or not
all Cubans wanted it.

Obviously, the prospect of independence did not necessarily enliven the
spirits of the Cuban Creoles. No other Spanish American colony depended so
heavily on African slave labor. The mainland colonies, with large Indian popu-
lations coerced to labor on Spanish haciendas and mines, had less use for
African slave labor. But the Cuban planters faced ruin without the enslaved
Africans. Of a population of 553,000 in 1817, nearly 200,000 Cubans were
African slaves. Another 114,000 blacks were classified as free persons of color.
That meant that whites were minorities in a predominantly black country, the
only such colony in the Spanish Empire. In addition, no other Spanish colony
experienced such a late colonial economic boom, and no other colony faced
such a grave threat of radical social revolution and racial war.

Religion, culture, language, class, and politics drove deep divisions among
the inhabitants of Cuba. While the Creoles continued to look toward Europe

for their inspiration, the Africans held fast to their own cultures, despite the inhumanity to which they had been subjected in the middle passage (the crossing of the Atlantic in wretched conditions on slavers), at the slave market, and on the plantations. The African Cubans preserved elements of their native languages, diets, musical tastes, and religions, so much so that they lived in a world far removed from the Creoles and the Peninsulars. In the slave quarters, beliefs and practices from different parts of Africa fused with elements of Spanish culture and Catholicism to produce a unique hybrid culture.

Examples of the emergent African Cuban culture were many. On Sundays, the African slaves on the plantations celebrated and worshiped in accordance with their own traditions, with their white masters occasionally joining the drinking, drumming, and dancing. The Yoruba beliefs of the Congolese people survived, despite the efforts of Catholic priests to suppress it. The African faithful assigned Christian counterparts to their own *orishas* (gods or goddesses). Santa Bárbara was also Chango, the African god of thunder, lightning and fire. The Virgin of Caridad del Cobre, the patron saint of Cuba, was also Ochún, the goddess of love and passion. Catholic priests might have taken some satisfaction in seeing the free black population of east Havana worshipping Our Lady of Regla, a black Madonna, but the proud Africans associated her with Yemayá, the mother of the sea.

These Africans, free and slave, shared few cultural traits and political ambitions with the Cuban Creoles. A cultural synthesis was being born, with elements of African and Spanish practices contributing to a unique sense of *Cubanidad* (Cuban nationalism), but the fusion was hardly evident in the aristocratic mansions on the outskirts of Havana or the slave quarters in central Cuba. Relations between Spaniards and Cubans, Peninsulars and Creoles, whites and blacks, aristocrats and the poor, remained tense and they had occasionally exploded in violence.

The Cuban Creoles recognized the extent to which their wealth depended on military power to maintain order in the colony. Without that power, social chaos, perhaps even racial war would result, compelling them to look to Great Britain, France, or the United States for protection. The Creoles knew that Great Britain and the United States valued the island for its strategic location and sugar plantations. Great Britain, however, having abolished the slave trade, would undoubtedly stamp out slavery in Cuba. The United States had terminated the slave trade as well, but slavery remained intact on its southern plantations. Consequently, the Creoles began to look favorably on the option of annexing their island to the United States in some fashion, compelled by the practical necessity of preserving their economic and political interests. As early as 1810, Creoles had proposed to annex their island to the United States. A liberal government had come to power in Spain and proclaimed the abolition of slavery. At that point, the Cuban planters began to plot the transfer of the island to the United States as a means of keeping the institution of slavery— and their own prosperity—intact. The scheme went nowhere, as did the liberal Spanish government, but the Creoles had begun to see a way out of their predicament. They did not yet realize that American interests did not fit so neatly into their vision of a Cuba free from Spain. From the rebellions of the vegueros, the slaves, and the growing grievances of the planters emerged a vague concept of an independent Cuba, but social, racial, and ethnic divisions within Cuba diminished its power and obstructed its growth.

Beyond Cuba, the strategic and economic ambitions of the United States also frustrated the political ambitions of the Cubans, including the planters. The North Americans valued Cuba for its strategic and economic value, but they shared the British disdain for Spanish Catholicism and their colonial subjects. They might have wished to annex Cuba, but they did not necessarily endorse the incorporation of Cuba as a state, a political status that would give equal representation to white Cubans in the U.S. Congress.

Prominent political leaders of the United States, from Thomas Jefferson to John Quincy Adams, favored the acquisition of Cuba by any means. The United States, having acquired Spanish Louisiana and Florida, wanted to expand across the continent to the Pacific. American merchants engaged in a profitable trade with Cuba and they wanted to increase trade there and throughout the Caribbean. Cuba was the key to that expansion. Jefferson referred to Cuba as "the most interesting addition which could ever be made to our system of states." The question was whether the United States would acquire Cuba by war, purchase, or Spanish default. American leaders preferred to wait for the latter, convinced that the acquisition of the island was inevitable. John Quincy Adams articulated this sentiment best, saying "Cuba, forcibly disjoined from its own unnatural connection with Spain, and incapable of self-support, can gravitate only towards the North American Union, which, by the same law of nature, cannot cast her off from its bosom."

The key phrase in this statement was that Cuba was "incapable of self-support." The specter of Haiti haunted the Americans, particularly Southerners, as much as it did the Cuban planters. And their American counterparts had no confidence in the ability of the Cuban planters—the descendents of Spanish aristocrats whom they loathed—to maintain order on the island. In short, the Americans were not prepared to tolerate another slave insurrection, and they feared a Spanish withdrawal from Cuba would trigger another vicious rebellion. The administration of President James Monroe, which supported independence for Spanish and Portuguese America—and even warned the powers of Europe not to attempt any further colonial ventures in the Western Hemisphere in the so-called Monroe Doctrine of 1823—actually favored the continuation of Spanish rule on the islands of Cuba and Puerto Rico, the last bastions of Spanish imperialism in the Americas.

The justification for this apparent contradiction in American foreign policy was that the United States opposed independence for an island society in which there was a majority of black or colored persons. Secretary of State Henry Clay explained this position directly: "The population itself of the island [Cuba] is incompetent at present, from its composition and amount, to maintain self-government." The fact that the Creoles seriously negotiated annexation proposals with a government that considered them incompetent demonstrates the depths of their fear, not their patriotism.

Simón Bolívar, the great liberator of South America, found no support in the United States for his plan to liberate Cuba and Puerto Rico. Spanish royalists and the remnants of the defeated Spanish armies retreated to the safety of Cuba, strengthening the pro-Spanish position of the planters and the Cuban military officers. After the humiliating loss of Havana to the British in 1762, the Spanish reformed the military system to provide more effective defense against foreign predators. Cubans served in the Spanish militia and Creoles gained command of the regular army on the island. By the time the wars for independence erupted on mainland South America, Cubans, not Spaniards, controlled the army. For the most part, the officers and the soldiers remained loyal to Spain, not just because they feared social chaos but because they were generally content with Spanish rule. They were in control of their own destiny and they had benefited politically and economically from the Spanish reforms of the late eighteenth century. They had little reason to seek a change in their political status, particularly when the available alternatives offered such little hope for stability or prosperity.

As the Spanish empire collapsed around them, the Creole planters in Cuba maneuvered their way through complex and turbulent times, at home and abroad. They promoted and defended their interests as best they could. As Spain's economic power declined, they engaged in free and open trade with English and American traders, including slavers. African slave labor, capital improvements, and open markets kept sugar production booming and the Creoles happy. For a few more decades, there would be little talk of annexation or independence. Economic prosperity continued, extracted from the hard labor of more than 200,000 slaves. The Creoles were reluctant to consider any political change that would slow the rate of growth, reduce their profits, or expose them to servile insurrection.

Nevertheless, the seeds of Cuba Libre had been planted in ground fertilized by the martyrdom of Hatuey, the protest of the vegueros, and the slave rebellions that punctuated the early nineteenth century. By the late nineteenth century, these seeds would grow into a powerful political movement, one nourished by a tradition of resistance to foreign oppressors.

CHAPTER TWO

The Wars
for Independence,
🌿 1825–1898 🌿

*C*arlos Manuel de Céspedes, a lawyer and sugar planter from eastern Cuba, had never been comfortable with Spanish rule over Cuba. As a law student at the University of Madrid, he was so active in antigovernment conspiracies that he was forced to return to Cuba in 1843, at the age of twenty-four. He opened a law practice in Bayamo and managed his family's sugar plantation, La Demajagua, but he remained a vocal critic of Spanish policy. He was arrested in 1851 for the crime of reciting an anti-Spanish poem. After the Glorious Revolution of September 1868 toppled Queen Isabella II of Spain, Céspedes seized the opportunity to strike for Cuban independence. On October 10, 1868, he assembled more than one hundred co-conspirators at La Demajagua and incited them to rebellion, declaring "the power of Spain is decrepit and worm eaten. If it still appears strong and great, it is because for over three centuries we have regarded it from our knees."

Céspedes and his followers were frustrated with efforts of Cuban leaders to negotiate a satisfactory political settlement with the colonial authorities. If they did not take to the field, the Cuban rebels feared that the Spaniards might impose a solution by military force. The planters and former slaves who gathered at La Demajagua concluded that rebellion was their only option. Céspedes boldly declared, "We only want to be free and equal, as the Creator intended all mankind to be . . . we believe that all men were created equal." He also advocated the "gradual, indemnified emancipation of slaves." With his moderate political manifesto, the *Grito de Yara* (the cry or shout of Yara, a town in eastern Cuba), Céspedes launched the first Cuban war for independence.

Two days later, after a skirmish with the Spanish army, Céspedes and his small army camped out at the Maceo family farm in Majaguabo. Marcos Maceo, a free black man born in Venezuela, and his mulatta wife, Mariana Grajales, sympathized with the rebel movement and fed the soldiers. Although they favored the immediate abolition of slavery without any compensation to the slave owners, the Maceos were prepared to fight with Céspedes for Cuban independence. Marcos gave the rebels some gold and guns, but his most valuable contribution to the rebel army was his son, Antonio. The young Maceo quickly distinguished himself as a strong and bold fighter, rising through the ranks of the rebel army to become the most accomplished and revered commander, known as the "Bronze Titan" of Cuban independence.

Other fighters, including Antonio's brothers, provided the military leadership and combat skills that Céspedes lacked. Máximo Gomez, a Dominican officer who had fought a guerrilla campaign against the Spanish army in his native country, also contributed his military leadership to the rebel army. By the end of 1868, Céspedes had 12,000 men in arms and controlled a handful of towns and farms in eastern Cuba.

For fifteen of the next thirty years, Cubans fought a bloody war against Spain to achieve their political independence. In the process, they also fought with each other to define the meaning of Cuba Libre. By the 1890s, José Martí had united Cuban patriots behind a political program that aimed to create a republic built on the fundamental principle of the equality of all Cubans—black, white, and mulatto. The struggle for Cuban independence begun with the politically moderate Grito de Yara became a revolutionary movement designed to restructure Cuban political, economic, and social life. To Martí, the war for independence was a war for national redemption. Cubans would have to fight to free themselves of Spanish tyranny and repent for the sins of slavery by creating a republic characterized by political independence, racial equality, and social justice.

SUGAR AND SLAVERY

Sugar and slavery spread across Cuba in the nineteenth century, bringing unprecedented prosperity to the planters and appalling misery to hundreds of thousands of African slaves. Slave traders in Africa packed the terrified captives so tightly into the holds of ships that they had no room to move. Wallowing in their own filth and chained to wooden platforms, they were fortunate to survive the voyage across the Atlantic. This traffic in human suffering, described as "the most odious wickedness that ever disgraced or afflicted mankind," brought 750,000 African slaves to Cuba between 1763 and 1862.

The slave traders unloaded their human cargo in the port of Havana and stored them in barracks located near the sumptuous gardens of the governor's summer palace west of the city. The elites of Havana could take a leisurely carriage ride along a tree-lined boulevard so that they might inspect their potential new "merchandise." While the other Spanish American countries had already abolished slavery, the Cubans held onto it dearly, unwilling to develop their economy without exploiting slave labor.

Cubans held onto slavery longer than any other country in Spanish America, but there were no other distinguishing features of Cuban slavery. The planters liked to claim that they treated slaves better than their North American or Brazilian counterparts did, but the high incidence of slave insurrections in Cuba belied this assertion. Africans fought for their freedom on sugar plantations in Puerto Príncipe, Holguín, and Trinidad in 1812; on sugar and coffee estates in Jaruco, Matanzas, Macuriges, and Havana in 1835; and on sugar plantations in Cienfuegos, Trinidad, Havana, Cárdenas, and Matanzas in 1840.

Occasionally, slaves and their white or mulatto sympathizers attempted to coordinate uprisings. In 1811, José Antonio Aponte organized a rebellion based in Havana, Puerto Príncipe, and Oriente. In 1843, three hundred slaves from fifteen different estates rose in rebellion in Matanzas. The frequency and ferocity of slave rebellion leaves little doubt that the life of a slave in Cuba was no better than the life of a slave in Brazil or the United States.

Most of the slaves who worked on Cuban plantations in the nineteenth century had been born free. With vivid memories of life as free men and women in Africa, they fought to recover their liberty. Most of the slaves were male, and many of them came from cultural groups with strong traditions of military service. The Cuban planters knew that only the whip would keep these Africans in bondage, and they applied it liberally. The most intractable slaves wound up in a special building in Havana in which torturers perfected their craft. If the slave master requested a *novenario*, the slave received nine lashes a day for nine days. If the slave had been particularly stubborn, the master might request the *boca abajo llevando cuenta*. In this particularly gruesome torture, the slave had to count the lashes aloud as he or she received them. If the victim made a mistake in counting, the whipping began anew. A month or two in the stocks would have been preferable to these punishments.

In response to the planters who claimed to practice a mild variant of slavery, the Africans and their historians could point out the unusually high rates of death (10 to 12 percent) among the slave population of Cuba. Indeed, the planters had to import so many slaves because the slave population on the plantations did not grow naturally. Life expectancy for a slave on many nineteenth-century plantations was less than seven years from the date of arrival. Brutal and inhumane work on the sugar plantations, combined with high rates of disease, illness, and malnutrition, combined to produce a harvest of death. The treatment of slaves on a sugar plantation in Matanzas and a coffee *finca* in Pinar del Rio might have differed somewhat, but slavery, no matter where it was practiced, dehumanized and killed people.

Nearly half of all African slaves, however, worked on sugar plantations, most of them in and around Matanzas, Cárdenas, Colón, and Santa Clara in central Cuba. During the six-month harvest, slaves often worked twenty-hour days, in the field as well as the factory. The foremen maintained a tight schedule because any interruption in the process threatened to ruin the harvest and the planter. The foremen sent gangs of slaves into the cane fields with machetes early in the morning and kept them working in the mills late into the night. The slaves were lucky to sleep four hours a day during the harvest. Wage laborers would not tolerate these working conditions, and the slaves did not either, but they could only challenge the system by fighting or fleeing it, both of which they tried often.

Spanish officials and Cuban planters tortured, imprisoned, and executed rebellious slaves and their associates. They had lived in fear of a Haitian-style slave rebellion for decades and crushed all conspiracies without mercy. When they picked up rumors of a plot to liberate 600,000 African slaves, they responded with such savagery that the widespread use of the ladder, as one popular form of torture was called, gave its name to the alleged plot, *La Escalera*. The torturer stripped a suspect and strapped him or her to the ladder by the wrists and ankles. One or two men stood over the victim with a bullwhip and flogged the exposed torso until the alleged conspirator started talking. If the person did not succumb in one session, he or she would be brought back the next day for another. Theodore Phinney, a sugar planter in Cárdenas regarded as too lenient with his slaves, watched in horror as one slave was tortured on the ladddder and asked, "Is it in the nineteenth century that we live?"

Indeed, it was 1844. Among the persons suspected of plotting rebellion was Gabriel de la Concepción Valdés, a poet known as Plácido. A light-skinned mulatto, Plácido was probably the most famous person of color on the island. In his poetry, he had dared to praise the spirit of Hatuey that animated thousands of strong and intelligent Cubans who suffered under slavery. Spanish authorities, however, were not moved by Plácido's display of an indigenous nationalism. They placed him in solitary confinement and interrogated him for days. Although he was spared the whip, he gave the names of fifty-five people associated with a plot. His confession did not save his life. On June 28,

1844, he was executed by a firing squad in Matanzas along with ten other convicted men.

The Creole aristocrats, resting comfortably in luxurious Havana mansions, hardly recognized Plácido or his followers as Cuban nationalists. Yet a separate Cuban identity was emerging, its cultural and political outlines shaped by rapid population growth, economic development, and immigration. The population of the island had doubled, from 553,033 in 1817 to 1,396,470 in 1862. The white residents of Cuba in 1862 now constituted a majority of the people. Their numbers had been augmented by the influx of French settlers from Haiti and white Spaniards fleeing the wars of independence in Santo Domingo or mainland Spanish America.

The city of Havana grew rapidly and expanded westward beyond the old city walls. By the 1860s, there were 140,000 people living in Havana and the city covered two square miles. To accommodate and facilitate the city's expansion, Captain General Tacón built a broad, tree-lined boulevard from the wall to the Castillo del Príncipe, near his luxurious summer residence. Along the broad avenues of the Paseo de Tacón (now known as Salvador Allende Avenue), the aristocrats built palatial estates known as *quintas*, far from the increasingly unpleasant barrios close to the harbor. The Creole planters wanted so much to be aristocrats that they purchased titles of nobility. It cost a mere $25,000 to become a count and $45,000 to become a marquis; these prices were so attractive that the Peñalver family purchased four titles and the Calvos picked up two.

The lifestyle and pretensions of these aristocrats depended mostly on sugar, but entirely on slave labor. Sugar production soared from 15,000 tons in 1790 to more than 720,000 tons in 1868. Cuba became the world's largest producer of cane sugar, replacing former British and French colonies in the process. Sugar mills proliferated, rising from 1,000 in 1827 to nearly 2,000 in 1868. The most productive mills, the highest concentration of African slaves, and the largest areas planted in cane could be found on the northern coast, from Matanzas through Cárdenas and Colón all the way to Sagua La Grande and Santa Clara inland. In this region, sugar planters cleared large tracts of forest, ignorant of and unconcerned by the environmental devastation they wrought in pursuit of profit. They imported steam-powered mills to increase productivity, and they looked favorably on railroad construction to boost exports.

The planters of eastern Cuba, however, did not share equally in the sugar boom. Eastern Cuba had been relatively less developed since the earliest days of the Spanish colony, and it fell further behind in the nineteenth century.

The planters of this region cultivated less land, bought fewer slaves, used oxen-powered mills, and produced less sugar than did their western counterparts. As the wealth and power of the western planters increased, the wealth and power of the eastern planters declined. Feeling isolated and neglected by the western planters and the Spanish authorities, the Creoles of eastern Cuba became even more hostile toward Havana. The free blacks of the region, who had long found refuge from the slave plantations in the mountains, added to the anti-Spanish feelings of the eastern Cubans.

Thus, the movement for Cuban independence originated in the east and spread westward across the island. The Havana aristocrats were not likely leaders of any movement to rid Cuba of Spanish rule and slavery. Despite some political grievances with the colonial authorities, their economic interests were not incompatible with continued Spanish rule. Although Spain had signed a treaty with England by which it had committed to end the slave trade beginning in 1820, the captain-general in Havana rarely enforced its terms. The result was that slavery survived long after the official termination of the slave trade. Unless and until Spain chose to enforce the treaty, slavery—and the prosperity of the sugar planters—would endure. If the Cuban planters demanded their independence, Spain could always liberate the slaves, a threat made explicit by the Spanish in the 1840s.

The Cuban leadership could not yet conceive of a free Cuba with free Africans. The rare and notable exception among the Creoles was Father Felix Varela. The first professor of philosophy at the Seminary of San Carlos in Havana, Father Varela represented Cuba in the liberal Spanish parliament in 1820–21. The failure of liberal reforms in Spain led him to call for the complete independence of Cuba and the abolition of slavery with compensation, two radical propositions that reflected a growing current of opinion among dissatisfied Creole intellectuals. Exiled to New York in 1823, Varela continued to promote his political views from abroad, in *El Habanero*, the dissident newspaper he published and smuggled into Cuba. In time, the Spanish authorities perceived him as such a threat that they sent assassins after the increasingly popular priest.

To most of the Cuban elites in the early nineteenth century, however, complete independence with abolition risked a massive slave rebellion. To those tired of Spanish taxation and absolutism, their first and best hope for a change in political status rested with annexation to the United States as a slave state. To that end, a group of Cuban planters formed the Club de la Habana in the 1840s. Led by Miguel Aldama, Cuba's wealthiest sugar planter, the club became the center of the Cuban annexationist movement, which also had its advocates in the United States. In 1847, two American champions of Cuban annexation, John O'Sullivan, editor of the *Democratic Review*, and Moses Yale Beach, editor of the *New York Sun*, met at the palace of Miguel Aldama to discuss strategy. Aldama wanted to preserve slavery, the basis of his fortune. O'Sullivan and Beach argued that the United States had a right and duty to expand beyond its borders. O'Sullivan, who had coined the expansionist credo "manifest destiny," came out of the meeting convinced that the Cubans preferred entry into the union rather than complete independence. He and Beach returned to the United States and persuaded President James Polk to offer Spain $100 million to purchase Cuba outright, just as the United States had bought Louisiana and Florida, former Spanish possessions.

Spain rejected Buchanan's offer, and the annexationists concluded that they would not get the island unless they took it by force. Narciso López, a native Venezuelan who was related to two members of the Club de la Habana, recruited soldiers in the southern United States for an expedition to liberate Cuba. López and his army of mercenaries attacked Cárdenas in 1850, believing that the locals would welcome them as liberators. The Cubans, however, fled to the hills rather than join the foreign invaders. López retreated, organized another expedition in the United States, and invaded Cuba a year later. This time the Spanish army quickly captured him and executed him by the garrote in the Plaza de Armas in Havana.

The planters gradually came to realize that Americans had a strong desire for Cuba but no great love for the Cubans. Generally, the American expansionists viewed both black and white Cubans as members of an inferior race, unfit for self-government. They did not really want to liberate Cuba as much as buy it. President Franklin Pierce raised the offer to $130 million in 1854. If Spain still refused to sell Cuba, what would the United States do? Three American diplomats offered one course of action in a frank declaration of imperial ambition known as the Ostend Manifesto, which stated that if Spain refused to sell (as it did), "then, by every law, human and divine, we [the United States] shall be justified in wresting it from Spain if we possess the power."

The American Civil War, ending with the abolition of slavery and the victory of the Union in 1865, ended all hopes for annexing Cuba to the United States as a slave state. The Cuban aristocrats then sought political and economic reform within the Spanish Empire. The Spanish government reciprocated by acceding to planter demands for more slaves. Despite treaty obligations and intense British pressure to abolish the slave trade, Cuba imported 90,000 African slaves between 1856 and 1860, the largest influx of slaves in any five-year period in Cuban history. In the 1860s, the Spanish once again indicated that they might accept Cuban representation in their parliament. Sensing a rare political opportunity, Cuban planters organized the Reform party in 1865. Led by former annexationists like Miguel Aldama, the party advocated tax reforms, representation in the Spanish parliament, and full equality between Creoles and Peninsulars.

Some of the Reformists even began to advocate the gradual abolition of the slave trade and ultimately slavery, a sign that they now recognized the futility of maintaining slavery in the face of strong British and American opposition. Moreover, Cuban planters were beginning to recognize that slavery was an unproductive and economically inefficient labor system, the bottom line being more important than moral calculations. Between 1844 and 1864, 140,000 Chinese workers arrived in Cuba as indentured servants. Free white laborers also arrived directly from Spain or the Canary Islands. Unlike slaves, these workers did not have to be fed, sheltered, and clothed year round. In the 1850s and 1860s some planters freed their slaves or allowed them to purchase their freedom. Rather than invest in slaves, this new group of entrepreneurs embraced wage labor and purchased machinery to increase productivity and profits.

With Cuban planters less attached to slavery and the slave trade, prospects for a political solution to their grievances with Spain brightened. The Spanish government allowed Cubans to elect representatives to a special committee to study Spain's colonial policies and recommend reforms. A dozen members of the Reform Party were elected and sailed for Spain in 1866. For a moment, it looked like Spain would be willing to adopt political and economic reforms that would satisfy the demands of Cuban reformists. Just before the Cuban representatives arrived in Madrid, however, a more conservative government came into power, one less inclined to accept Cuban proposals. The Cubans pressed their case to an unsympathetic government until the committee adjourned in April 1867, having accomplished nothing. The reform movement ended, and with it the hopes for peaceful change evaporated.

THE TEN YEARS WAR, 1868–1878

From Spain the conservatives attempted to repress the reformist movement in Cuba. The captain-general, now directly subordinate to Spain, silenced the opposition press, banned political meetings, and exiled his critics. In 1867, Spain raised income taxes and imposed a higher tariff on Cuban imports. The United States retaliated by raising taxes on Cuban products by 10 percent, a measure that inflicted serious damage on the Cuban sugar industry, still reeling from a decline in sugar prices that hit a low in 1866. The combination of political reaction, new taxes, and economic recession reminded planters of the most onerous aspects of Spanish colonialism.

The wealthiest planters of western Cuba had a chance to survive the political and economic crisis of 1867 and 1868, but the relatively weak planters of eastern Cuba did not. Their decline had already begun, and if they did not find a way to modernize their operations, these new taxes and tariffs threatened to ruin them. Their welfare, however, was of little concern to the Spanish captain-general in Havana because they produced less than 10 percent of the island's total sugar crop. Eastern Cubans, neglected by both Spanish bureaucrats and Havana-based planters for decades, began to see rebellion as the only viable means of promoting their general interests. They had little to lose and much to gain by liberating Cuba from Spain and slavery.

For all the economic grievances that united the planters of eastern Cuba, they lacked a common political agenda. Soon after Céspedes declared Cuba's independence, other planters contested his leadership and ideology. A faction led by Ignacio Agramonte opposed the concentration of civil and military authority in the hands of Céspedes. Rebel representatives assembled at Guáimaro in April 1869 to draft a constitution, form a provisional government, and establish rebel policies. Although Céspedes was elected president of the republic in arms, General Manuel Quesada was appointed commander in chief of the rebel army. More important, the delegates established policies that reflected the interests of Cuba's planter elite. Any slave who joined the rebel army would be free. Other slaves were freed as well, but they had to continue working for their masters, who were obligated to pay, feed, and clothe them. To those who advocated immediate abolition, like Antonio Maceo, the rebel government's position on slavery fell far short of their demands.

Even worse, the provisional government subsequently declared itself in favor of annexation to the United States. A group of planters led by Miguel Aldama was in fact lobbying in Washington toward that very end. Annexation had failed before and it was destined to fail again if the Cubans did not abolish slavery immediately. The wealthy planters nevertheless saw annexation as a practical means to maintain political stability and economic productivity. President Ulysses S. Grant refused to meet the Cuban representatives, however, not wanting to antagonize Spain. The Grant administration, like so many before and after it, preferred to purchase Cuba rather that see it liberated by the Cubans. If Spain could not suppress the rebellion and restore order, the Grant administration was prepared to intervene, not to free Cuba but to replace

Spanish with American government. The United States would not even recognize the Cuban rebel government as a legitimate belligerent, a legal status that would have allowed the Cubans to purchase arms and supplies in the United States.

Deep divisions between radical and conservative factions of the rebel movement further weakened the cause. Conservative planters, namely Céspedes, Agramonte, and Salvador Cisneros Betancourt, wanted an alliance with the wealthy planters of western Cuba and the United States. To get that alliance, they had to compromise on the issues of slavery and independence. More radical members of the movement, namely Máximo Gómez and Antonio Maceo, firmly opposed any compromise on these issues. They wanted to enlist former slaves and free blacks into their rebel army, and to recruit them they were prepared to abolish slavery and destroy the plantations. They would accept nothing less than full independence and immediate abolition. If the rebel movement fought for annexation to the United States, Maceo said he would fight with the Spaniards against the rebels.

The divisions within the rebel government affected the military strategy of the rebel army. Gómez, who commanded rebel forces in Oriente Province, recognized that the key to victory lay in the disruption of the sugar industry and the abolition of slavery, both of which provided Spain with the revenues it needed to prosecute the war. Moreover, abolition would bring thousands of African men into the rebel army. The planters were reluctant to embrace such a radical strategy, fearing not only the loss of productivity but also a racial war that might result from immediate emancipation. Therefore, Gómez never took the rebel army very far into the western provinces.

The rebellion was essentially confined to eastern Cuba, partly by the design of the rebels, and partly because of Spanish defenses. The Spanish built a fortified trench across the narrowest portion of Cuba, a thirty-mile stretch of land between Júcaro on the southern coast to Morón on the Atlantic. Gomez crossed this trench, known as *la trocha*, in January 1875, after he destroyed eighty-three plantations in six weeks, freeing the slaves. His western rampage, however, alarmed the rebel planters as much as it did his Spanish opponents. In April, a new rebel assembly dominated by conservatives stopped Gómez's invasion of the west while the conservative leaders reconsidered their military strategy. They were particularly concerned about the political ambitions of General Antonio Maceo, Gómez's most aggressive field commander. The Spanish authorities charged that he intended to set up a black republic, a rumor that few Cuban leaders were inclined to believe. Meanwhile, Gómez and Maceo kept pressing for an invasion of the west, but the conservatives held them in check. As a result, the great sugar plantations in Matanzas, Cárdenas, and Colón remained in full production, virtually untouched during ten years of warfare, and hundreds of thousands of African slaves remained in bondage.

The conservatism of the civilian leaders shackled their own army in eastern Cuba, a result that played into the hands of the Spanish military. Sensing an opportunity to crush the rebels, the Spanish captain-general, Arsenio Martínez Campos, launched a military offensive in 1877 with a well-equipped and disciplined army of 70,000 men. He drove the rebels east of the trocha and quickly gained the advantage. To induce the rebels to capitulate, he offered a general amnesty to all who agreed to leave the island. The conservatives, exhausted by ten years of war, agreed to terms in the pact of Zanjón of 1878. This truce did not include any provisions for Cuban independence or abolition; it merely offered the rebel leaders safe passage out of Cuba and amnesty for all soldiers. Only slaves and Chinese servants who had fought in the rebel army would gain their freedom.

General Martínez Campos recognized, however, that the acquiescence of General Maceo was the key to forging a real and lasting peace. He met with the general, who had suffered twenty-one wounds in ten years of combat, at Baragua in March 1878. He hoped to persuade Maceo to accept the terms of Zanjón, but Maceo did not want to hear anything of an armistice that did not provide for abolition or independence. The Spanish general protested, saying that he would not have agreed to the meeting if he had known that Maceo would insist on those two points. Maceo still commanded 1,500 troops, and there was no doubt that he would continue fighting. As a courtesy to an enemy officer, Martínez Campos asked him how long he might need before hostilities would resume. General Maceo stated bluntly: "I do not find it inconvenient that they break out right now." Cooler heads prevailed and hostilities began again eight days later.

The first war for Cuban independence essentially ended with an indecisive truce in 1878. Maceo vowed to fight on, but he could not. Cuba had been ravaged by ten years of war. More than 200,000 Spanish soldiers had paid the ultimate price to defend Spanish colonialism; perhaps 50,000 Cubans had died fighting it. Financial support for the war was not forthcoming, and Maceo's comrades had capitulated. Maceo left Cuba for Jamaica in May 1878, having salvaged a measure of honor in his denunciation of Zanjón, known as the Protest of Baragua. Because of one heroic act, Cuban patriots could later claim that they had only accepted a temporary cease-fire in 1878.

As if to prove it, Generals Calixto Garcia and Antonio Maceo organized an uprising the next year. But the *Guerra Chiquita* (Little War, 1879–80) ended

soon after it began. The tenuous peace between Spanish royalists and Cuban patriots prevailed. The leadership of the rebels, exiled throughout the Caribbean and
the United States, continued to plot insurrection, while important political and
economic forces changed the nature and direction of the Cuban independence
movement.

BETWEEN WARS, 1878–1895

After the Ten Years War, the Cuban sugar industry faced challenges almost as
dangerous to its maintenance as were the rebel armies. Competition from
other sugar producers, such as Hawaii, compelled the Cuban planters to modernize their operations. To rebuild mills destroyed during the war and finance
their modernization projects, the planters had no choice but to borrow money
from people in the United States. Others could not afford the costs of recon-
struction and sold their properties to United States companies. North American businessmen and bankers moved into the sugar industry and eventually
displaced the Cuban planters. They acquired mills and plantations once owned
by the Cuban aristocracy and began to transform the sugar industry. The foreign owners mechanized refineries, putting the oxen-driven mills out of business. Cuban planters continued to cultivate cane, but they became increasingly dependent on the large, American-owned refineries to grind the cane
and market the refined sugar abroad. By 1895, United States investment in
Cuba had reached $50 million and trade with Cuba exceeded $100 million,
greater than the total amount of American trade with the rest of Latin America.

Cuba, for all practical purposes, had been converted into an economic
dependency of the United States, though it was still politically subordinate to
Spain. U.S. trade with and investment in Cuba exceeded that of Spain and
every other European power. The Cuban planters, even the most productive
ones in the western provinces, exercised less control over markets and policy.
They now had to contend with both Spanish and American policies and objectives, neither of which necessarily coincided with their own. Their economic grievances combined with a growing sense of national identity to revive the cause of Cuba Libre, but the new American presence threatened to
truncate the life of any independence movement. If the Cuban patriots did
not win a quick and decisive victory on the battlefield, sovereignty over Cuba
might soon pass from the Spanish to the Americans. The United States, which
had sat out the first war for independence, would not likely sit on the sidelines
in any future conflict. As long as Spain maintained the order and stability that
U.S. investors demanded, the United States would not challenge Spanish au-

thority. If that authority collapsed, however, the U.S. government would find it difficult not to intervene, regardless of the will of Cuban nationalists.

Before 1868, the leadership of the Cuban rebellion would have welcomed U.S. intervention. During the Ten Years War, however, powerful revolutionary leaders like Máximo Gómez and Antonio Maceo developed an uncompromising commitment to complete independence. From the United States they asked only for the recognition of their rights as belligerents. Their nascent anti-imperialist and nationalist convictions found full expression in the person and ideology of José Martí, who emerged as the civilian leader of the Cuban independence movement in the early 1890s.

Born to Spanish parents in Havana in 1853, Martí was too young and frail to fight in the first war, but he was arrested for criticizing the colonial government and exiled to Spain in 1871. He was destined to live the rest of his life away from the country he yearned to liberate. He traveled throughout Europe, Latin America, and the United States over the next twenty-four years, spending most of his time in New York, where he earned a living as a journalist and got involved in the political activities of the Cuban exile community. As brilliant with the pen as Maceo was with the machete, Martí expressed a utopian vision of an independent Cuba that coincided with and reinforced the republican aspirations of generals Maceo and Gómez.

Slavery had come to a gradual end in the 1880s, as the Spanish had intended through the Moret Law of 1870. Although this law freed only slaves over the age of sixty and the children of slaves, it also terminated the slave trade, which meant that slavery would die with the last African slave on the island. Many Cuban planters saw the inevitable end and freed their slaves to rid themselves of an economic burden. In 1886, Cuba finally abolished slavery, the last Spanish American country to do so.

As in the rest of the Americas, abolition did not mean the elimination of racism and oppression in Cuba. Africans and Chinese continued to work long hours on plantations for meager wages, and they faced discrimination, neglect, and abuse from their former masters. Martí envisioned a Cuba free of racial hatred and conflict, a sovereign nation that represented all Cubans. Spanish colonialism, Martí recognized, was only part of a larger problem. The internal divisions that had weakened the first war for independence, differences between rich and poor, black and white, east and west, men and women, had to be bridged to make Cuba a strong, independent, prosperous, and virtuous society. The rebellion, when it came, would not be fought just to protect the property and interests of the white Cuban elite. In fact, the rebellion would constitute a democratic revolution, for Martí advocated a political system built on the principles of racial equality, social justice, economic independence, and political liberty. For him, the purpose of the war was larger than the establishment of an independent nation: it would be a war for national redemption.

Martí realized that the previous war, led by the Creole planters, lacked the popular support needed to organize an army and keep it in the field. The independence movement would not succeed, he argued, if he and his compatriots did not propose an ambitious political program that offered real reforms to Cubans of color, most of them peasants and workers. The independence movement gained momentum thanks to Martí's successful appeals to the working-class communities of Cuban exiles in Key West and Tampa in the 1890s. Key West had emerged as a cigar-manufacturing town in the 1860s, after the United States raised taxes on imported Cuban cigars. To avoid the taxes in their largest market, the Cuban cigar manufacturers set up factories in the United States. Thousands of Cubans followed the factories, first to Key West and then to Tampa. The workers in these two factory towns pushed forward a political agenda calling for complete independence along with social and economic reform. Martí built the Cuban Revolutionary Party (PRC) on a working-class foundation of the exile communities in the United States, changing the social base and ideological orientation of the independence movement.

Under Martí's leadership, the PRC provided discipline, direction, and an ideology to the independence movement that the prior insurrectionists had lacked. Under Martí's leadership, the call for Cuba Libre came to represent a political movement and an ideology, a call to arms to achieve complete independence with universal justice. Many others had articulated the rationale for independence, but none of them ever organized a broadly based political coalition that crossed class, race, and gender lines. Thousands of Cubans formed clubs in New York, Philadelphia, Key West, Tampa, and Jacksonville, and they too gave meaning to the cause. Under the umbrella of the PRC, Cubans in the United States raised funds, gathered supplies, and organized expeditions to resume the war for independence. Gómez, Maceo, and Calixto García, seeing the miraculous organizational work being done by Martí and the PRC, answered the call to arms when the PRC issued it on February 24, 1895.

THE CUBAN WAR FOR INDEPENDENCE, 1895–1898

The Cuban War for Independence began with a whimper in 1895, not the bang of an American invasion in 1898. Spanish agents learned of the PRC's plot and crushed the rebellion in western Cuba before it got off the ground. Martí's plans to invade the island with a force of more than one thousand soldiers had been scuttled in January 1895, when the United States seized three vessels loaded with arms at Jacksonville, Florida. Martí, the civilian leader, and Gómez, the general in chief, landed in eastern Cuba in April, followed shortly thereafter by Maceo, second in command. Just as the leaders were beginning to organize the Cuban Army of Liberation, Martí rode into a Spanish ambush on May 19 and was killed instantly. With his death, the revolutionary movement lost the leader who had unified the movement with a revolutionary ideology and clear political direction.

The war continued under the military command of Gómez, a native Dominican who shared Martí's ideology if not his political charms. Yet the movement had been united and institutionalized through the PRC, allowing the rebels to survive the loss of its most articulate spokesman. Nearly 60,000 Cubans joined the rebel army, more than half of whom were black or mulatto. With 40 percent of the commissioned officers men of color, black officers commanded white soldiers in the field, making the army of liberation unique in the annals of Western military history. The peasant soldiers, known as *mambises*, often marched into battle with only a machete, but they fought superior Spanish forces in every province of the island.

The Spanish responded with their typically desperate and defensive tactics. They strengthened the trocha in a vain attempt to confine the rebellion to the eastern provinces. They cleared a swath of land one hundred yards wide and constructed a railroad line down the center to transport troops to any point penetrated by the rebel armies. With garrisons, lookout posts, barbed wire, and electrical lighting along its length, the trocha presented more of a psychological than a military obstacle. If the rebels crossed it and invaded the western provinces, they would change the character and purposes of the war. It would mean incorporating former African slaves en masse; it would mean fighting for something more than just the replacement of Spanish Peninsulars with Cuban Creoles.

Salvador Cisneros Betancourt, the conservative former president of the provisional government, was reelected president by the rebel assembly in September 1895, but military strategy was the responsibility of Gómez and his lieutenant general, Antonio Maceo. On November 29, Maceo crossed the trocha in forty minutes without a single casualty. On the western side of that supposedly impenetrable barrier, Maceo joined forces with Gómez, who had also crossed without any losses. With a combined force of 2,600 men, the invading army prepared to take on nearly 100,000 regular Spanish troops and

60,000 volunteers. The Spanish, however, were stretched thin, having to defend plantations, mills, railroads, and fortifications across the island. Under Gómez's leadership, the rebel forces pursued a classical guerrilla strategy, striking quickly against vulnerable portions of the Spanish army, rarely presenting themselves to the superior Spanish forces in the open field.

On January 1, 1896, the *Diario de la Marina* of Havana reported that the rebel army had retreated to eastern Cuba. In fact, Maceo and the invading army had on that very day entered Havana Province. Captain General Martínez Campos resigned a week later, replaced by the hard-line General Valeriano Weyler. Determined to pacify the entire island at whatever cost, General Weyler on February 17 ordered all rural inhabitants to reconcentrate into fortified Spanish towns within eight days. Any person caught outside the concentration camps would be considered a rebel sympathizer and summarily executed. The infamous reconcentration order forced hundreds of thousands of Cubans into poorly prepared camps, wherein they died in much greater numbers than they did in the field.

Weyler's reconcentration policy only increased the determination of the Cuban rebels, particularly the officer he feared most, General Maceo, who had marched his army to the westernmost tip of the island. Then he made camp in Pinar del Río Province, almost in plain view of the Spanish army. Weyler had assigned 60,000 troops to the pursuit of Maceo, who defied his enemy for a year. As he rode into battle on December 7, 1896—bearing twenty-four scars of battle wounds, testimony to twenty-eight years of fighting—a bullet struck him in the face and knocked him out of his saddle. A second bullet struck him in the chest, and the Bronze Titan finally came to rest.

The war, however, dragged on for another year. The Spanish herded an estimated 300,000 Cubans into concentration camps, where they died of hunger and disease by the tens of thousands. Weyler, "The Butcher," had brought total war to the island, forcing civilians to choose between the concentration camps and the liberated territory of the rebel army. Cuban patriots chose the latter and the rebel army grew powerful enough to fight the superior Spanish army to a stalemate for most of 1897. The Spanish rested securely in their forts and cities, while the Cuban army camped in the countryside. Neither army possessed the strength to defeat the other, but in a war of attrition the Cubans would eventually defeat the Spaniards.

The plight of the victims of Weyler's concentration camps was brought to the attention of the American people by the newspapers in graphic reports that magnified the atrocities of the Spaniards and the heroism of the Cuban rebels. Many Americans came to sympathize with the Cuban rebels, having read stories of Spanish perfidy and inhumanity in the popular "yellow press" of the time, sensationalist and fiercely nationalistic papers such as William Randolph Hearst's *New York Journal*. Partly in response to public opinion hostile to Spain, the United States government kept a watchful eye on the war in Cuba. During the presidential election campaign of 1896, Republican candidate William McKinley accused the outgoing president, Grover Cleveland, of doing nothing about the crisis in Cuba. His opponent, William Jennings Bryan, opposed popular calls for American expansion. McKinley won the election and, shortly after his inauguration in March 1897, warned the Spanish government that if Spanish troops or diplomats could not resolve the Cuban conflict, the United States would do it for them.

Cuba possessed an economic and strategic importance that McKinley could not ignore. More than 90 percent of Cuba's exports went to the United States, and most of its imports came from the United States. Moreover, prominent policymakers, intellectuals, and businesspeople had been advocating for an aggressive foreign policy to protect American power abroad. The United States had recently completed its expansion across the continent, eliminating indigenous resistance in the western territories and acquiring new land and resources. Theodore Roosevelt, assistant secretary of the navy in the McKinley administration, and Henry Cabot Lodge, Republican senator from Massachusetts, argued that the United States, the world's leading industrial power, now had a responsibility to protect and promote American commercial expansion. Because the war in Cuba threatened American trade and property on the island, expansionists like Roosevelt and Lodge argued that the United States had the right and duty to intervene, militarily, if necessary.

By the end of 1897, Spanish authority had nearly collapsed. Weyler had concentrated about 300,000 Cubans into the camps, and he had 200,000 regular Spanish troops under his command, yet he could not crush the rebel army. The Spanish attempted to resolve the conflict by offering political autonomy to Cuba, but General Gómez would stop for nothing short of complete independence. He grew confident that his army would defeat the Spaniards on the battlefield. In January 1898, Gómez reported from Las Villas that the Spanish army was in complete retreat. "This war cannot last more than a year," he predicted optimistically.

The explosion of the U.S.S. *Maine* in Havana harbor on February 15, 1898, changed the course of the war. President McKinley had dispatched the battleship to Havana in late January with Spanish approval, after rioters in Havana protested the installation of the new autonomist government. The yellow press reported the riots as a sign of mounting public unrest that Spain could not control, and intensified its calls for American military intervention. The war that McKinley still hoped to avoid became inevitable when, on the night of February 15, a massive explosion sank the *Maine*, killing 260 sailors. Theodore Roosevelt blamed the wreck on Spain's "dirty treachery." At the time, nobody knew exactly why the ship exploded, but jingoistic Americans accused the Spanish of sabotage and howled for a declaration of war against Spain. An investigation conducted by U.S. admiral Hyman Rickover in the 1970s produced conclusive evidence that the explosion that sank the *Maine* had been caused by an internal coal fire, not a Spanish mine.

The combative and expansionist Americans did not, however, need hard facts to justify war against Spain. The McKinley administration could no longer ignore increasingly popular demands for war, although it did offer to purchase Cuba from Spain for $300 million, thereby resolving the conflict by transferring the island to the United States. Spain rejected the offer, of course, which had not been made with the advice or consent of the Cuban leadership anyway.

The United States would now accept nothing less than an end to the war on its terms. For a mixture of humanitarian, economic, and strategic motives, the United States intervened to restore order and stability. This did not necessarily mean that the Americans would grant independence to Cuba. Since the presidency of James Monroe, U.S. policy had been based on the assumption that Cubans were unfit for self-government. Thus, when the United States declared war against Spain on April 25, there was no mention of Cuban independence as a goal of the action. President McKinley simply authorized the use of force to terminate hostilities between Spain and Cuba, and to establish a stable government on the island. In the Teller Amendment to the declaration of war, Congress disclaimed any interest in annexing Cuba to the United States, but the Cubans would get control of their government only after the Americans decided that they could manage their own affairs.

With the entrance of the United States, the Cuban War for Independence was transformed into the Spanish-American War. General Gómez, his army camped out in central Cuba, hoped the Americans would join his forces in a combined assault on Havana. The United States Army, however, was determined to fight the Spaniards on its own, with the racially integrated Cuban army units serving as auxiliaries, not allies. The American generals dismissed Gómez as irrelevant and ignored his plan to take Havana. After assembling in Tampa, 17,000 U.S. troops invaded eastern Cuba in late June, with the forces of Lieutenant General Calixto García covering their landing. The Spanish fleet was anchored in nearby Santiago harbor, and the American army determined to crush it. The Americans moved quickly to achieve their own objectives, without consulting the Cuban officers or their provisional government. The American entry into the war was beginning to look more like an intervention than a liberation.

As it happened, the American army quickly defeated a Spanish army and navy fighting only to salvage their honor. The only significant land battle occurred on the heights overlooking Santiago, where African American soldiers led the charge up San Juan Hill while Teddy Roosevelt's Rough Riders took the adjacent Kettle Hill. Shortly thereafter, America's new ironclad fleet destroyed the Spanish fleet as it made a desperate run out of Santiago harbor. With that, the war ceased. Spanish generals signed an armistice with the United States on August 12, 1898. No representative of the Cuban government participated in the negotiations. Calixto García's army was not even allowed to march into Santiago to celebrate the victory. In December of that year, the Spanish-American War formally ended with the Treaty of Paris.

With an American army occupying Cuba, Máximo Gómez refused to attend the ceremonial flag raising at Morro Castle because the stars and stripes was raised over Havana. "Ours is the Cuban flag, the one for which so many tears and blood have been shed," he explained. In thirty years, the struggle for independence had claimed the lives of more than 400,000 Cubans and Spaniards. Gómez urged Cuban patriots to band together to "end this unjustified military occupation." With the American general residing in the Palace of the Captain General, rebel leaders had to reflect on an uncertain future, captured in a prophetic question of Martí: "Once the United States is in Cuba, who will get it out?"

CHAPTER THREE

The First Republic,
❧ 1898–1934 ❧

*T*he citizens of Havana anxiously gathered at the Plaza de Armas to observe the lowering of the Stars and Stripes from the Captain General's Palace. Triumphal arches towered over the narrow streets of old Havana, bearing portraits of Martí, Maceo, and other patriots. Flags hung from balconies, and bands marched through the streets playing the national anthem. At noon on May 20, 1902, General Leonard Wood, the American governor-general of the island, would finally transfer political authority to Tomás Estrada Palma, the first Cuban president of independent Cuba. Although the president's powers would be limited by treaty, many Cubans did their best to believe that the moment for which they had waited more than thirty years had arrived.

The palace, overlooking the entrance to Havana harbor, had been the seat of Spanish authority for nearly four hundred years, and the center of American authority for the past four. The Americans had occupied the island with a force of 40,000 troops—twice the size of their invading army of 1898—while they decided Cuba's political status. In the declaration of war in April 1898, the United States had disclaimed any interest in permanently occupying or annexing Cuban territory. The McKinley and Theodore Roosevelt administrations, however, were not eager to grant absolute independence to Cuba. The Cuban leaders, previously praised as heroic patriots, allegedly still could not govern themselves. If they gained control of Cuba, Americans feared that anarchy would spread across the land. In the most charitable assessment of Cuban incompetence, American leaders explained that the Cubans lacked education and experience in public service. At worst, the Americans charged that the Cubans were no better prepared for independence than "the savages of

Africa." The commanding general of the American army, William R. Shafter, claimed that the Cubans were "no more fit for self-government than gunpowder is for hell."

Unless and until the Cubans provided the United States with guarantees that they could form a stable government capable of protecting America's vital strategic and economic interests, the United States army of occupation would not leave. Many Americans believed that the right of conquest gave them the right and duty to determine Cuba's future. What would happen to American interests on the island if a rival power such as Germany invaded a free Cuba? What would happen if a free Cuban legislature passed a law expelling American companies from the island? Few American leaders were willing to sail away from Havana with nothing, and they neither sought nor welcomed advise from Cuban leaders. The political reality was that the United States would not grant independence to Cuba if the Cubans did not recognize the right of the United States to protect order and stability on the island.

Many Cuban political and military leaders, however, demanded full sovereignty, and some were even prepared to continue fighting for it. Critics of American expansion in the United States also opposed the annexation of Cuba and advocated an immediate withdrawal from the island. The United States government ultimately imposed a compromise solution. Cuba would receive a conditional independence, unlike Puerto Rico and the Philippines, which remained under direct U.S. administration. To protect its vital interests, the United States insisted that the Cubans accept the terms of an amendment introduced by Senator Orville H. Platt of Connecticut. The first two clauses of the Platt Amendment of 1901 limited Cuba's rights to negotiate treaties with foreign powers and borrow funds abroad. The third provision gave the United States "the right to intervene for the preservation of Cuban independence, the maintenance of a government adequate for the protection of life, property, and individual liberty." In effect, the Platt Amendment would turn Cuba into a protectorate of the United States, a nominally independent country under the guidance and protection of its powerful northern neighbor.

The Platt Amendment drove deep divisions within the Cuban leadership. The Cuban representatives to a Constituent Assembly convened by General Wood rejected the amendment by a vote of 24 to 2 on April 6, 1901. They then sent a delegation to Washington to negotiate a compromise agreement that would respect Cuba's rights as an independent nation. President McKinley however, insisted that the American troops would not be withdrawn if the Cubans did not accept the Platt Amendment verbatim. On June 12,

1901, the Constitutional Convention accepted it by a vote of 16 to 11, with Salvador Cisneros Betancourt, former president of the republic in arms, voting against it.

The McKinley administration got what it wanted and proceeded with plans to hold elections and form an acceptable Cuban government. Tomás Estrada Palma emerged as the preferred candidate of the United States and the conservatives of Cuba. He had lived in New York State for twenty years, and the former revolutionary had lost much of the rebellious energy that once animated him. Bartolomé Masó, another former president of the republic in arms, emerged as the strongest opponent of Estrada Palma. With the backing of many former military commanders, Masó attempted to campaign as an uncompromising opponent of the Platt Amendment. General Wood informed Washington that radicals, particularly black Cubans, had enthusiastically endorsed Masó. In a transparent attempt to rig the elections, General Wood appointed only Estrada Palma men to the oversight committee to supervise the election and count the ballots. Masó withdrew from the election, charging that Washington had rigged the first free elections in Cuban history.

Cubans thus approached the inaugural ceremonies of May 20, 1902, with conflicting emotions of pride and sadness, hope and anger. For some notable independence leaders it was a bittersweet moment, and they regretted that they had disbanded the army of liberation and the Cuban Revolutionary Party. Others, like president-elect Tomás Estrada Palma, repeatedly offered thanks to the Americans for agreeing to withdraw their troops and grant Cubans their independence, albeit limited by the Platt Amendment.

In any case, the presence of General Máximo Gómez at the inaugural ceremonies conferred legitimacy on the proceedings. Gómez, who had refused to participate in the ceremonial raising of the American flag four years earlier, had come to the palace to raise the Cuban flag over Havana for the first time. General Wood began the ceremonies at noon by reading a letter from President Roosevelt. The former Rough Rider declared the occupation at an end and expressed his best wishes for peace, prosperity, and enduring friendship with Cuba. After reading the letter, General Wood lowered the American flag. Then, he and Gómez raised a red, white, and blue flag with a single white star. One eyewitness reported that "it was the crowning moment of Máximo Gómez's life when he raised the flag of his long devotion over the palace, the nerve center of Spain's power in the island." Tears streamed down the general's face as he raised the flag over Cuba Libre.

THE POLITICS OF THE FIRST REPUBLIC, 1902–1933

President Estrada Palma inherited a nation decimated by thirty years of war. The population of Cuba had declined from 1.8 million in 1895 to 1.5 million in 1898. Agricultural production had collapsed. Only 207 of 1,100 sugar mills survived the war, and 800 tobacco vegas, 700 coffee fincas, 3,000 livestock ranches, and more than 100,000 small farms had also been destroyed. Fortunately for Cuba, Estrada Palma presided over four years of relative peace and good government.

The political order broke down in the presidential election campaign of 1905. General José Miguel Gómez, representing the Liberal party, attempted to challenge Estrada Palma's bid for a second term. Gómez withdrew his candidacy and charged that the president was attempting to fix the elections and intimidate his opponents. As a result, Estrada Palma won a second term in another uncontested election, but this time his opponents cried foul and prepared for revolt. On August 16, 1906, the Liberals rose in rebellion led by Pino Guerra and Orestes Ferrara. Estrada Palma, with no regular army to contest the Liberals, asked President Roosevelt to dispatch American troops to quell the rebellion. Roosevelt, already preoccupied with interventions in Panama and the Dominican Republic, was reluctant to intervene. The resignation of Estrada Palma on September 28 left Cuba without a government and Roosevelt without a viable alternative. On September 29, two thousand U.S. marines landed outside of Havana and Secretary of War William Howard Taft established a provisional government.

Just four years and four months after the first American occupation of Cuba ended, another one had begun. Cuban political leaders had failed in their first effort to establish a republican government. The electoral fiasco of 1906 and the rebellion that followed clearly demonstrated the pernicious influence of the Platt Amendment on Cuban politics. Not only did it sanction U.S. military intervention, it encouraged Cuban politicians to request such intervention in pursuit of their political ambitions. Estrada Palma and the conservatives he represented might have expected the intervention to support their cause; the Liberals expected the intervention to bolster their claim to the presidency. The Platt Amendment, promoted as a means of guaranteeing Cuba's political stability, served to destabilize Cuban politics. A Platt Amendment mentality took hold in Cuban and American politicians, characterized by cynicism and disillusionment about the nature of

Cuban independence and the prospects for stable and effective self-government.

The second American occupation began in 1906 under Charles Magoon, appointed governor of Cuba after a stint as governor of the Panama Canal Zone. During his three-year tenure, Magoon attempted to placate the growing rift between the Liberal and Conservative parties by bringing representatives of each into the growing bureaucracy. Although the origins of the two major parties were in the civilian and military wings of the independence movement of the 1890s— the former more moderate in its political positions than the latter—both groups had lost ideological substance by the end of the second American occupation. Now, the two parties represented personalistic factions of the political elite, each of them more concerned about winning presidential elections than implementing reforms. Control of the government meant an opportunity to distribute patronage in the form of government offices, through which the Cuban leadership could then accumulate wealth through graft and extortion. Martí's principle of "with all, and for the good of all," already was a distant memory, a dream shattered by avaricious Cuban politicians.

The opportunities for graft soared after 1898, as American investors moved into all sectors of the economy and displaced the Cuban elite from their traditional positions in command of the sugar industry. The lack of economic opportunities in the private sector lured the Cuban leadership into the public sector, increasingly seen as an attractive and lucrative career option. Under Estrada Palma, the public payroll expanded to 20,000 employees, and the expansion of the bureaucracy continued under Governor Magoon. By 1911 the public payroll had expanded to 35,000 employees, with government salaries representing as much as two-thirds of the government budget. Thus, the presidential elections during the First Republic represented opportunities to gain the right to distribute high offices to friends and associates. Historian Hugh Thomas described the political parties as "gangs of friends and pursuers of spoils rather than advocates of principle, ex-generals turned politicos who were exhausted by war and determined to share in the plenty of peace."

As corruption spread throughout the bureaucracy, public cynicism about public service spread with it. A public administrator could hope to gain wealth by taking bribes from foreign companies seeking a concession to build a road or acquire a license. Graft, bribery, and embezzlement, not the national good, became the goals of public servants. Perhaps the most lucrative source of funds was the national lottery, established in 1909. The president of the republic, as well as senators and representatives, could augment their regular salaries through the sale of lottery tickets. A senator alone could supplement his salary by as much as $54,000. For these leaders, public service became more lucrative than private enterprise. Corruption polluted the entire political environment. As much as 25 percent of government revenue was lost to corruption every year.

During the administrations of liberal José Miguel Gómez (1909–13) and conservative Mario Menocal (1913–21) nearly four hundred indictments were brought against public officials for embezzlement, fraud, misuse of public funds, and violations of electoral laws. There were no real ideological differences between the political parties. Former military heroes squandered their good reputations in search of personal wealth. Mario Menocal, a general in the Army of Liberation, came into the presidency with a fortune of $1 million and left it in 1921 with $40 million.

To the Cubans of color, the degeneration of politics in the First Republic meant more than just public malfeasance. To them it meant that they had fought in vain for Cuban independence *and* social justice, for they had gotten neither. Black Cubans left the field of battle looking for land and jobs, knowing that they had earned the rights to full and equal participation. Aside from a few influential leaders like Juan Gualberto Gómez and Martín Morúa Delgado, Cubans of color did not assume politically significant roles in the republican governments. The lack of political opportunities added to their mounting frustration over the general lack of economic progress since the abolition of slavery. In fact, in eastern Cuba, with the highest percentage of blacks in the country, economic conditions deteriorated. Many officers and soldiers of the Liberation Army had settled in eastern Cuba after the war, where land was abundant and cheap. As American investors descended on the region to build railroads and sugar mills, however, they were moved off the land. The loss of land hit the black Cubans particularly hard in the Guantánamo river valley, east and north of Santiago, where they constituted a majority in several municipalities. The region had come under the control of North American sugar companies, who wanted the black Cubans as workers, not competitors.

Persons of color dissatisfied with the Liberal and Conservative parties formed the *Partido Independiente de Color* (PIC, Independent Party of Color) in 1907 to push for greater political and economic opportunities. White and black Cubans denounced the PIC, arguing that it was unpatriotic to organize any party along racial lines, citing the dictum by José Martí that there were no whites, blacks, or mulattos, only Cubans. Senator Martín Morúa, one of the most influential black Cubans, introduced legislation that banned all political parties organized along racial lines. In turn, the PIC criticized the Morúa law and lobbied for its abrogation. Evaristo Estenoz, leader of the PIC, demanded greater participation in the republic for all Afro-Cubans. But the established leaders saw in Estenoz and the PIC a new threat of a race war, a fear that had existed since the late eighteenth century. Thus, when Afro-Cubans associated with the PIC revolted in Oriente Province in May 1912, the government responded with a ferocity reminiscent of the *Escalera* conspiracy.

The rebellion began as an organized political protest against the Gómez administration, with a specific demand to repeal the Morúa law, but it quickly became a serious rebellion supported by as many as 10,000 black Cubans in Oriente Province. The insurgents directed their anger at property owners, particularly the foreigners who had built railroads, plantations, and sugar mills in the province. To protect American interests in eastern Cuba, a contingent of U.S. Marines landed near Santiago on May 31. President Gómez then declared martial law and dispatched Cuban troops to root out and destroy the rebels. The rebels knew they could not engage the Cuban army on the battlefield, so they split into small bands and dispersed across the countryside. The Cuban troops hunted down and executed rebels and all suspected sympathizers. In this sweep, they killed as many as three thousand black Cubans, almost all of whom were denied the courtesy of a trial. The brutal tactics worked. There would never again be a revolt organized along racial lines. It would not, however, be the last time American troops would intervene in Cuba. The next such landing occurred in 1917, during a liberal revolt triggered by the fraudulent reelection of Mario Menocal.

In short, politics in the First Republic revolved around the corrupt political interests of two political parties dominated by a white elite, with presidential elections triggering violence every four years. The Platt Amendment, by making American interventions legal, made them inevitable. The result was an unstable republican system of government characterized by fraud and corruption so pervasive that the Cuban political leadership lost all semblance of legitimacy. Cuba's political leadership shared some of the responsibility for the political instability as well, for they did little with their first opportunity to demonstrate that they could govern themselves.

THE DANCE OF THE MILLIONS

For their part, American investors took full advantage of Cuba Libre. One could even argue that American investors were the primary beneficiaries of independent Cuba. The Reciprocity Treaty of 1903 served as the economic counterpart to the Platt Amendment, confirming Cuba's status as an economic dependency of the United States. The treaty reduced American taxes on imports of Cuban products, particularly sugar, and lowered Cuban taxes on imports of American manufactured products in return. Cuba's role in this economic system was to export primary products like sugar, coffee, and tobacco and import all of its manufactured products from the United States. The treaty discouraged Cuban attempts to diversify the economy by promoting industrialization. Cubans had gained a limited degree of political independence, only to lose a large degree of their economic independence.

In material terms, the short-term results of Cuba's new economic relationship with the United States were impressive. American capital moved in to rebuild the sugar industry, purchasing lands and mills valued at more than $50 million by 1905. With preferential access to the American market serving as a stimulus to the investors, sugar production increased steadily, exceeding the 2-million-ton mark for the first time in 1913. Cuba was then producing 12 percent of the total world supply of sugar, accounting for most of the sugar consumed in the United States market. Thanks to the Reciprocity Treaty of 1903, Cuban sugar drove all European and West Indian competitors out of the American market.

Non-Cuban companies, however, now produced most Cuban sugar. By 1905 United States firms owned 60 percent of all rural properties in Cuba; Spaniards owned another 15 percent. Cuban ownership of rural property had been reduced to 25 percent. Foreign companies took control of the sugar industry, bringing in modern machinery to increase production. The American investors also turned their attention to eastern Cuba, an area that had been underdeveloped in comparison to the great sugar-producing regions of Matanzas and Las Villas in the nineteenth century.

The United Fruit Company (UFCO) of Boston, founded in 1899 by Andrew Preston and Minor Keith primarily to market bananas, recognized the value and potential of Cuban sugar and purchased properties in and around Nipe Bay on the Atlantic coast of Oriente Province. By 1905, with sugar prices and production soaring, UFCO had in Cuba 25,000 acres planted in cane, 4,440 head of cattle grazing on 15,000 acres, 100 miles of private railroad track, 17 locomotives, and 640 cane wagons. During harvest time, the company employed 5,000 people. "This investment," according to Hugh Thomas, "was the emblem of the time, the symbol of a North American penetration of the last Spanish dominion in the New World."

It also represented the new organizational features of the Cuban sugar industry. Whereas most nineteenth-century sugar producers cultivated sugar on their own lands and processed the cane in their own primitive mills, the mechanization and modernization of the industry that came with the American investors drove out many small and primitive mills. In the twentieth century, huge sugar refineries known as *centrales* came to monopolize the processing of sugar cane. These firms, almost all of them foreign owned, purchased cane from smaller planters, known as *colonos*, who had no alternative but to sell their cane to the centrales for processing because they could not afford to purchase the machinery to refine their own sugar. Among the colonos who sold cane to the UFCO mills was Angel Castro, a Spanish immigrant and the father of a son named Fidel. Like other colonos, Angel Castro made a decent income from sugar cultivation, but he depended on a foreign-owned central to purchase and market his sugar.

Cuban dependency on the United States and its citizens was cemented by North American investment in infrastructural development. In 1900, William Van Horne and Percival Farquhar formed the Cuba Company to complete the railway line from Havana to Santiago. To Van Horne, the founder of the Canadian-Pacific Railway line, the construction of a line from Santa Clara in central Cuba to Santiago was a relatively minor task with potentially high profits. The Cuba Company soon laid the tracks that linked the new sugar plantations and mills of eastern Cuba to the line. In 1911, the American financial stake in the Cuban railway system was valued at $25 million, the second largest American investment on the island.

Tobacco also came under American domination. Cuban growers continued to cultivate tobacco and their expertise was invaluable to the industry, but American-owned companies manufactured and marketed at least half of all Cuban cigars and cigarettes after 1898. In 1899 the Havana Commercial Company of New York bought twelve cigar factories in Havana, but the American Tobacco Company acquired it in 1902, part of a larger process of consolidation in which the American Tobacco Company bought another twenty factories. By 1902, 50 percent of the highly esteemed Cuban cigars were manufactured in factories owned by North Americans.

Americans also invested in utilities, banks, ports, communications, mining, and manufacturing. By 1911, American investment on the island had reached $200 million, more than twice the combined value of British, French, and German capitalists. Foreign investors displaced the planter class, modernized key industries, and fashioned an economic dependency that would last for decades. Cubans exported their sugar and tobacco to the United States; they imported manufactured products from the United States. The Cuban economy could grow only as a reflection of the continued health and vitality of the American market, and as long as Americans purchased Cuban products and sold Cubans the manufactured goods they needed, the economy apparently prospered.

World War I provided another impetus for a surge in sugar production. With European producers out of the market, Cuba expanded its share of world output. A steady increase in sugar prices during and immediately after the war created an unprecedented boom in sugar profits. The price increased from 1.9 cents per pound in 1914 to 9.2 cents per pound in February 1918, the highest price sugar had ever reached. To the delight of the sugar planters, the price continued to soar all the way to a record price of 22.5 cents on May 19, 1920. The sugar barons had never dreamed of selling so much of their sugar at such high prices. Cuba was in the midst of what was called the "dance of the millions," a sugar mania that gripped the entire country as the sugar harvest of 1920 peaked at a record value of $1 billion in 1920, twice the value of the 1919 harvest.

The dance of the millions stopped soon after it began. After the war, European sugar producers re-entered the market and suddenly there was more than enough sugar to satisfy world demand. Prices dropped as quickly as they had risen, hitting 11 cents in late October and sliding all the way down to 3.75 cents by Christmas. During the frenzy, many sugar producers had taken out loans to finance improvements on their properties, demonstrating that the bankers shared their confidence in the future of Cuban sugar. Few anticipated the decline would come as quickly as it did, which spelled disaster for many. When the sugar boom went bust, many planters and bankers found themselves overextended or out of business. With their economic prospects suddenly diminished, a few began to question the wisdom of concentrating scare resources on a single sector.

The crisis exposed the weaknesses of what many analysts have labeled a classically dependent economy. The economy of the republic, dependent on the export of primary commodities such as sugar and tobacco, boomed when Americans and Europeans were willing and able to purchase Cuban products, none of which were essential commodities. If and when the market collapsed, the Cuban economy faltered. Because much economic policy was shaped by the Reciprocity Treaty and global market conditions over which the Cuban government had no control, the republican government was powerless to prevent or even ameliorate the affects of the economic depression that followed the dance of the millions.

Cuban workers received an unequal share in the prosperity that came with the sugar boom, and they were the first to feel the impact of the post–World War I depression. Employment in the sugar mills and fields was seasonal and wages were low even during the harvest season. Sugar workers were typically unemployed or underemployed, and the fact that sugar prices soared during a brief period of time had not substantially altered their wages or employment patterns. Beyond the sugar industry, the economic crisis that followed the economic bust affected workers everywhere. Factory owners, trying to cut costs in order to stay in business, shut down operations and dismissed workers.

Not everybody shared equally in the benefits of economic development, and the workers wanted a larger share of it. To defend their interests, railroad workers, cigar makers, stevedores, miners, and others organized to promote their cause, which meant an increase in pay and better working conditions. In an effort to unite workers across the country, a national congress was held in 1914. As the sugar barons danced with their millions, the working classes organized for action, enraged that foreigners and a minority of Cubans hoarded the profits of an unprecedented economic boom. As 1920 approached, strikes and work stoppages throughout the island corrected the illusion of a blanket of prosperity created by the sugar boom.

Workers convened in Havana for a second labor conference in 1920, the climactic year in the sugar industry. Delegates from 102 unions, representing some 90,000 workers, passed resolutions calling for an eight-hour workday, equal pay for men and women, public housing, and government assistance. The government, controlled by a political elite closely associated if not subservient to American interests, turned a deaf ear to the workers' demands. But the workers would not be so easily dismissed. Their calls for social and economic justice resonated throughout the republic, expressing popular dissatisfaction with political leaders who no longer endorsed Martí's plans for a redemptive revolution.

Women also organized for the right to participate equally in the First Republic. José Martí had said little about the rights of women in the ideal republic, leaving the impression that the utopian society he wanted to create would be a republic led by and for men. Yet women had fought alongside men in the wars for independence and organized patriotic clubs to support the cause. Despite their contributions, women did not gain the right to vote or serve in public office. Men attempted to confine women to the home, but the economic realities of the time meant that more and more women had to enter the labor force. The number of working women increased from 66,000 in 1899 to over 89,000 in 1919.

At the same time, women organized to press for their political rights. In 1915, women formed a suffrage party to lobby for the right to vote. A Feminist Club of Cuba was founded in 1918 to promote civil and social rights for women. Like the workers, women presented a challenge to the political authorities, for they demanded a voice in government as well as social and economic reforms. In 1921, women organized the National Federation of Feminine Associations to coordinate the efforts of several professional groups working for women's rights. This federation convened the first National Congress of Women in Havana in 1923. The resolutions passed by this congress reflected a general demand for substantial reform. Women called for equal rights under the law, the right to vote, and increased educational opportunities for women. Over the next ten years, women, workers, Cubans of color, students, industrialists, and the urban middle class presented increasingly militant challenges to the leadership of the First Republic and their American benefactors.

CUBANIDAD

A new generation of Cubans came of age during the 1920s. Born after the wars for independence or remembering little of the struggle, this generation learned of Cuba Libre as an unaccomplished ideal. Their Cuba was a protectorate and an economic dependency of the United States, not the ideal republic of which Martí had dreamed—that much was certain. Yet their Cuba was also vibrant and vivacious, allowing for and even generating new cultural expressions. As the politicians strayed far from the ideal, popular Cuban culture continued to flourish as ordinary men and women defined and developed a national identity.

The rush of corrupt presidents and American generals through the palace hardly seemed to matter. Far from Havana, from the villages around Santiago, through the cattle ranches of Camagüey Province, and across the fertile plains of Las Villas and Matanzas, *Cubanismo* took root and Cubans became more thoroughly Cuban. The development of a national identity grew from deep roots that originated in Africa, Spain, and the United States. Even as American influence became more noticeable in the Vedado and Miramar neighborhoods in Havana, a distinct Cuban identity could be heard in the sounds of *son* and *rumba* wafting out of the nightclubs in Habana Vieja and Marianao. The same social groups that were excluded from the centers of political and economic power during the First Republic created this national identity through art, music, sports, and literature. This sense of Cuban identity then found political expression in labor unions, student groups, women's organizations, and new political parties.

Nothing represented Cubanismo better than son, a music and dance form that originated in eastern Cuba in the late nineteenth century. On the outskirts of Baracoa and Guantánamo, the heart of the 1912 rebellion, black musicians developed a unique sound using African instruments like the bongó, maracas, and claves along with European instruments such as the guitar and trumpet. The syncopated bass rhythms characteristic of son inspired a music and dance craze that swept westward across the island and beyond. By the late 1920s, son had become a national and international music and dance phenomenon. It was, and still is, the most frequently heard music in Cuba, the "Cuban musical genre par excellence," according to music historian Robin Moore.

The political leaders initially attempted to suppress the infectious African rhythms, lyrics, and religious beliefs that infused son, the precursor of modern salsa. The middle and upper classes in Havana associated the music with the degenerate and unsophisticated black masses. Those who danced to son left their inhibitions at the door, gyrating to the rhythms in sensuous moves that some considered immoral. In 1913, some festive residents of Old Havana were dancing to son in their courtyard late in the evening when policemen showed up bearing nightsticks to put a stop to the spread of such scandalous behavior. Six years later, ten people in Guanabacoa were arrested for "dancing the immoral son." The police even confiscated the instruments of the musicians, being especially concerned about the bongó, which they associated with African/Cuban religions such as Santeria and abakuá.

Nonetheless, the sounds of son marched ever onward, through the dance halls and brothels and even to the streets of New York City. During the golden era of son (1920–40), famous groups such as the Septeto Habanero played at La Tropical beer gardens in Marianao, where a black and white middle-class culture flourished. Son became so popular that the white upper classes eventually adopted it as a national cultural symbol. If they did not want to be seen in public swinging their hips, they held private *encerronas* (lock-ins) and partied for days behind closed doors. In May 1925 President Gerardo Machado gave a formal endorsement to the dance craze by having the Sonora Matancera play at his birthday party. Son was now a beautiful expression of the new Cubanidad. Novelist Alejo Carpentier wrote that son "is a product unique to us, as authentically Cuban as any danza or bolero."

Writers and poets, historians and sociologists, cane cutters and cigar makers, all debated questions of national identity. As they searched for and exalted manifestations of a unique cultural identity, they helped to define Cubanidad, giving real meaning to the abstract concept of independence. At the University of Havana, Fernando Ortiz studied Cuban folklore and African religions and gave nonwhite Cubans a sense of pride in their contributions to Cuban civilization and culture. Jorge Mañach, a leading intellectual and a biographer of Martí, criticized the leaders of the republic not so much for accepting the Platt Amendment but for not taking responsibility for defending Cuban sovereignty. Nicolás Guillén gave intellectual and artistic voice to black Cubans through his poetry, exerting a powerful influence over a cultural and literary movement that demanded a greater part for persons of color in Cuban society. The decade of the 1920s was a period of cultural effervescence, with energetic debates giving life to literary magazines and journals such as *Revista Bimestre Cubana, Cuba Contemporanea,* and *Revista de Avance.* Some of Cuba's intellectual leaders organized the *Grupo Minorista* to provide a forum for the discussion of cultural renewal and national redemption. The Minoristas represented the voice of a new and restless generation, one critical of American intervention, frustrated in their political ambitions, and adamant that Cuban leaders return to the original principles of Martí.

The University of Havana campus emerged in the 1920s as fertile ground for the cultivation of innovative and even radical political and social ideals. Inspired by the Mexican and Russian Revolutions and more directly influenced by the university reform movement growing out of Argentina, the University of Havana students promoted a cultural resurgence that reflected the perspectives of a discontented urban middle class. In 1923 Julio Antonio Mella organized a student occupation of the campus and demanded that the political leaders recognize the autonomy of the university and offer free and universal education. That same year Rubén Martínez Villena and twelve other students walked out of a literary function to protest the attendance of a corrupt government official. The incident, known as the Protest of the Thirteen, soon became a general indictment of official corruption and malpractice. In 1927, the politically active and ambitious university students organized the *Directorio Estudiantil Universitario* (DEU, University Student Directorate) to promote educational and political reform. In the years to come, the DEU would play a pivotal role in national politics.

By all outward appearances, Cuba and Havana in the 1920s seemed to be a nation and a city enjoying prosperity brought about by relative peace and stability. Surrounding the University of Havana rose a neighborhood of marble palaces and interior gardens known as Vedado. Built during the years of the *vacas gordas* (fat cows) after the turn of the twentieth century, this neighborhood west of old Havana reflected the eclectic tastes and cultural ambitions of the old elite as well as a new generation of entrepreneurs. Those who could afford to do so imported paintings, sculpture, and furniture for their grand homes, where Cubanidad found few architectural expressions. The elites preferred large mansions built in European styles, fenced in by iron gates that separated them from the commoners who lived in old Havana, Cerro, and Marianao.

In a sense, there were many Cubas emerging during the early twentieth century. Vedado represented only one Cuba, a place of affluence that American investors and tourists came to know and love. But just a ferry ride across the channel brought one to another Cuba, the predominantly black community of Regla. In this poor neighborhood, the benefits promised in a new Cuba had never been realized: the debates about the Platt Amendment or the Reciprocity Treaty were essentially irrelevant. Cubans of color had fought for Cuban independence in greater numbers than had light-skinned Cubans; yet from the Cuban government they received virtually nothing. Esteban Montejo, a former slave, described the desperate straits of the Afro-Cubans: "After the war ended, . . . the Negroes found themselves out in the streets—men brave as lions, out in the streets. It was unjust, but that's what happened. There wasn't even one percent of Negroes in the police force."

The cultural ferment of the 1920s, built on solid Afro-Cuban foundations, produced a volatile public arena in which the political and economic leaders of the First Republic would contest the meanings of Cubanidad. The generation of 1895, the leaders of the First Republic, had squandered their opportunity to lead the nation, their credibility undermined each time they dipped into the national treasury. Confusing their personal enrichment with the prosperity of a nation, they could hardly recognize the conflict brewing even within the comfortable confines of Vedado. They had no idea how the people in the countryside lived and suffered, but anybody who cared to travel beyond Havana could not have ignored the great distance that separated the elites in Havana from the peasants in Pinar del Rio or the cane cutters in Oriente. Before the dance of the millions and after it, the majority of Cubans endured high rates of illiteracy, unemployment, underemployment, and infant mortality. These same Cubans were giving life to Cubanidad through cultural expressions such as son, but they did not participate in or benefit equally from the First Republic.

THE REVOLUTION OF 1933

There had been many rebellions and armed protests in Cuba during the First Republic. The Veterans' and Patriots' Movement of 1923, however, was different. The veterans of the wars for independence had been complaining about their treatment ever since the peace of 1898. Pensions were in arrears. Jobs and land were scarce. Most veterans felt that the First Republic had not fulfilled their dreams or compensated them for their sacrifices. To these grievances the generation born after 1898 added their criticisms of government corruption and economic dependency. The malcontents of the two generations merged in the Veterans' and Patriots' Movement of 1923. Led by old veterans like General Manuel Sanguily, the movement also attracted young people who would play important roles in the political life of Cuba over the next three decades, including Julio Antonio Mella, cofounder of the communist party, and three future presidents, Carlos Mendieta, Dr. Ramón Grau San Martín, and Federico Laredu Bru.

A political manifesto issued by the movement in August 1923 called for the purification of the government and its moral rectification, threatening revolution if the government failed to renovate the republic. The demands of the old generation and the new called for a free and fair press; women's political rights; the eradication of illiteracy; better working conditions for Cuban laborers; and an end to government corruption. President Alfredo Zayas (1920–24) refused to negotiate with representatives of the Veterans' and Patriots' Movement, condemning the group as seditious and banning its activities. A poorly organized and ill-fated uprising began in April 1924 and quickly fell apart. The leaders surrendered easily, going into exile or prison, and the threat of mass insurrection disappeared. To the younger leaders, the veterans showed a lack of conviction if not courage. If the young men and women wanted to purify the republic, they would have to do it on their own.

The traditional Liberal and Conservative parties lost their political legitimacy and moral authority during the regime of Gerardo Machado (1924–33). Elected as a Liberal on a "Platform of Regeneration" that called for a national revival, Machado did not turn out to be anything like a national redeemer. He recognized the calls for reform coming from a broad array of nationalist forces, particularly the students and a modernizing faction of the Cuban elite who saw their future tied to economic diversification and industrialization. In his first term as president, Machado actually delivered on some of his promises. A Customs-Tariff Law of 1927 provided tariff protection to industrialists who needed relief from foreign competitors to expand Cuba's small manufacturing sector. In addition, the construction of the Central Highway provided badly needed competition to the foreign-owned railroads and strengthened the country's transportation infrastructure.

If Machado had continued to play by the rules of the republican game, he might have satisfied the demands for reform. His successes, however, encouraged him to seek broader and deeper powers for a second term. Instead of just seeking reelection, he assembled a constitutional convention packed with his supporters, passed an amendment that abolished the vice presidency, and extended his presidency for another six-year term. The Liberal, Conservative, and Popular parties accepted the arrangement, known as *cooperativismo*, and endorsed Machado's uncontested election to a six-year term ending on May 30, 1935. With this electoral maneuver, Machado became a dictator and killed the democratic pretensions of the First Republic.

The Wall Street crash of October 1929, coming just five months after Machado's inauguration as a dictator, triggered a political and economic crisis in Cuba. The United States responded to its own crisis by erecting protective barriers around its battered economy, which only intensified Cuba's crisis. The Hawley-Smoot Tariff Act of 1930 raised duties on Cuban sugar, thereby reducing Cuba's share of the American market from 49 percent in 1930 to 25 percent in 1933. Sugar production dropped by 60 percent, and the Cuban economy went into a tailspin. Tobacco exports also dropped, from $43 million in 1929 to $13 million in 1933. Hard hit employers responded by slashing wages, firing workers, and closing factories. Soon, some 250,000 Cubans found themselves out of work. Those who kept their jobs had to accept lower pay. In the sugar fields, cane cutters had to accept a paltry twenty cents for a twelve-hour workday. The depression devastated Cuba.

Machado responded the only way that he knew, with repression. He sent assassins to Mexico to kill Julio Antonio Mella, the communist leader who had sought safety in exile. He banned all demonstrations by political parties or groups not legally registered. At a political rally organized by the Unión Nacionalista in May 1930, the army fired on a crowd of thousands. At the University of Havana, the DEU prepared to confront the regime in a massive protest on September 30. The police moved in to disperse the demonstration and, in the violence that ensued, killed Rafael Trejo, president of the Law School. Thereafter, the DEU waged war against the Machado regime, and the University of Havana became a battleground. On January 3, 1931, the police arrested twenty-two students for conspiring against the government. The next month, the police arrested eighty-five professors on charges of sedition, including Dr. Ramón Grau San Martín, a distinguished physiology professor. Each arrest and crackdown only seemed to encourage the student activists, whose demonstrated bravery conferred on them a moral authority that other opposition groups lacked. The students, part of the so-called Generation of 1930, assumed a primary role in the bloody struggle to overthrow the dictator.

The students were not the only ones fighting against the Machado regime. The dictatorship faced opposition on several fronts simultaneously, including factions within the middle classes and the army, both of them previous supporters. In October 1931, Dr. Joaquín Martínez Saenz, a middle-class lawyer, organized the ABC Revolutionary Society to fight the dictatorship. With its membership consisting of young professional men and women, lawyers, doctors, teachers, engineers and others, the ABC attacked the dictator with terrorist tactics of their own. On September 28, 1932, the ABC assassinated Senate President Clemente Vásquez Bello near the Havana Country Club. Machado responded in kind, unleashing his secret police (known as the *porra*) against the ABC, the DEU, and a more militant faction of the students known as the Student Left Wing. The porra hunted down and killed opposition leaders, leaving their bodies on the streets to terrorize the dictator's enemies into submission. The police broke into homes at night, arrested opposition leaders, and tortured them in dark cells. The victims were often "shot while trying to escape," a typical Latin American method of dealing with political opponents.

Violence continued to escalate in 1932 and 1933, bringing Cuba to the brink of outright civil war. In the countryside, sugar workers responded to the political and economic crisis by taking matters into their own hands, organizing strikes and demonstrations as well as occupying several mills. The Communist party of Cuba, organized by Julio Antonio Mella in 1927, was trying to organize the Cuban proletariat and assume the leadership of the anti-Machado movement, and it had some success. With or without the communists, Cuban workers in the countryside were organizing. In December 1932, sugar workers formed the National Union of Sugar Workers to press their demands. For the first time in Cuban history a labor union had gained a foothold in the countryside, a development that forced Machado and the United States to take serious notice.

Fearing that Cuba was once again teetering on the edge of anarchy, President Franklin D. Roosevelt dispatched Assistant Secretary of State Sumner Welles as a special ambassador to Cuba. Roosevelt wanted to resolve the crisis without resorting to military intervention, for he had just announced a Good Neighbor Policy based on the principle of nonintervention in Latin American affairs. Welles attempted to mediate the conflict between Machado and his opposition, with the threat of intervention looming over a deeply divided society. The DEU denounced his efforts as a new form of American intervention and refused to participate in any negotiations. Other groups participated in the mediation, including the ABC, but it quickly became apparent that any solution to the crisis had to begin with Machado's departure.

In early August, a strike begun by bus drivers and streetcar workers in Havana paralyzed the city. Under the leadership of the *Confederación Nacional Obrera de Cuba* (CNOC, National Confederation of Cuban Workers), and the Communist party, the strike threatened the stability of the regime. The CNOC represented 200,000 workers, and the Communists wielded significant influence over the labor unions. Strikers clashed with the police on the streets of Havana on August 7, leaving dozens killed and injured. With a social revolution apparently brewing, Welles intensified the pressure on Machado to resign. Machado's position became untenable on August 12, when army officers informed him that he would have to resign to save Cuba from American intervention or revolution. He resigned that night and fled to the Bahamas, leaving behind a provisional government led by Carlos Manuel de Céspedes, the son of Cuba's independence hero.

Three weeks later, on September 4, 1933, an unprecedented political alliance of students and disgruntled noncommissioned army officers led by Sergeant Fulgencio Batista deposed Céspedes and installed a provisional revolutionary government under the leadership of Dr. Ramón Grau San Martín. The students had struggled for years to redeem the Cuban republic. The sergeants, corporals, and enlisted men that followed Batista had originally intended to negotiate only for better pay and housing. Yet both groups suddenly found themselves in the presidential palace, from which they could remake Cuba. Thus, the revolution of 1933 began with idealistic officers and reformers hoping to purge the republic of its many shortcomings as they created a new Cuba.

The revolutionary government of Ramón Grau San Martín began with massive enthusiasm but ended in humiliating defeat one hundred days later. Grau represented the reformist ambitions of the Generation of 1930, middle-class students and professionals determined to break with the political traditions of the First Republic. Grau's main ally in the revolutionary government was his minister of interior, Antonio Guiteras, a twenty-seven-year-old former student leader with such power that many regarded the new government as a Grau-Guiteras coalition. Guiteras, an incorruptible socialist known as the man with only one suit, had led an anti-Machado guerrilla band in Oriente Province in 1933. Grau, a moderate reformer, was not without his political flair. On the day of his inauguration, he repealed the Platt Amendment.

The Grau-Guiteras government, the first independent Cuban government formed without the express approval of the United States, carried out sweeping reforms under the banner of Cuba for the Cubans. The government dissolved all traditional political parties, lowered utility rates, granted women the right to vote, and gave the university autonomy. A new ministry of labor would implement a series of labor reforms, including an eight-hour day, workers compensation, and a new requirement that Cuban workers had a right to 50 percent of the jobs in any enterprise.

These reforms struck hard at the pillars that supported the First Republic, and old Cuba responded in kind. Representatives of the old political parties did not just roll over and accept their abolition without a fight. Former president Mario Menocal returned to Cuba and attempted to maneuver his way back into power. Even some of the anti-Machado groups, particularly the ABC, challenged Grau from the right. Most significant, high-ranking officers opposed to Batista and Grau threatened to undermine the new government. They resented Batista, now a colonel and army chief of staff who controlled the army. Three hundred army officers opposed to Batista established a base of operations on the top floors of the Hotel Nacional, Havana's finest. On October 2, 1933, Colonel Batista ordered an assault on the hotel without consulting President Grau in advance. He took the hotel, arrested the officers, and thereby demonstrated his ability to maintain order.

The reform-minded students and their nominal allies in the army had united only to depose Machado. Faced with opposition at home and abroad, their political coalition began to disintegrate. The United States had refused to extend diplomatic recognition to the regime, a clear indication that it would look favorably on a change in government. With the Grau-Guiteras government barely able to control its own supporters, the United States sensed a serious threat to its political and economic interests in Cuba. Ambassador Sumner Welles went even further, asserting that the Grau-Guiteras government was "frankly communistic." Cuba once again teetered on the verge of civil war or anarchy.

Although FDR opposed another military intervention, he dispatched a naval fleet to Havana, a clear sign that he would act if the Cubans failed to create a government able to protect American interests. Batista, maneuvering his way through months of political turbulence, finally realized that the United States wanted *somebody* to form a stable, pro-American government. On January 13, 1934, Batista asked Grau to resign. Grau refused. Three days later, Batista declared Colonel Carlos Mendieta the new president of Cuba. Within a week, the United States recognized the provisional government Batista had created. Several months later, the United States signed a new treaty with Cuba that did not include the Platt Amendment, although by a separate lease the United States retained Guantánamo Bay, forty-five square miles of land and water, for use as a naval station.

Although the revolution of 1933 failed miserably to live up to the highest aspirations of Grau and Guiteras, it did give birth to a new republic. The leadership of Cuba passed from the generation of 1895 to the generation of 1930, and the Platt Amendment no longer restricted Cuban independence. The rescission of the Platt Amendment did not, however, eliminate the overwhelming American political, economic, military, and cultural presence in Cuban affairs or change the fundamental nature of Cuba's relations with the United States. Batista, a former army sergeant, aborted the revolutionary movement on behalf of American interests, knowing that the United States opposed the Grau-Guiteras government. By overthrowing Grau, Batista won the support of the United States, but he also frustrated and angered the growing number of adherents to Cubanidad, nationalists who expressed their independence in politics, art, literature, music, and sports. This generation of 1930, like the generation they displaced, found their nationalistic and reformist ambitions crushed again by a limited American intervention. From the rubble of the frustrated revolution of 1933 would emerge more radical and militant political movements; these would threaten to do much more than simply recognize the rights of women and workers.

PHOTOGRAPHS
CHAPTERS ONE AND TWO, 1492–1898

Top: Morro Castle in a storm, ca. 1910. Built in the sixteenth century to defend Havana against frequent pirate attacks, it was taken by the British in 1762. Courtesy Library of Congress, LC USZ62-966600.

Bottom: Cuba's Heroes. Lithograph used for promotional purposes at the Grand Cuban Fair, May 25–30, 1896. From top left: Máximo Gómez, Antonio Maceo, José Martí (center), Calixto Garcia, and Salvador Cisneros Betancourt. Courtesy Library of Congress, LC USZ62-101602.

Opposite top: Mambi Soldiers. More than 50 percent of the sodiers in the Army of Liberation were Cubans of color, many of them former slaves. Courtesy Library of Congress, LC-B2-2548-11.

Opposite bottom: Santiago Cathedral. Santiago, the first capital of the colony, declined in importance as Havana became the center of Spanish power. Author's Collection.

Above: José Martí on the steps of the Ybor Cigar Factory, Tampa, 1893. The Cuban exile communities in Key West, Tampa, New York, Jacksonville, and elsewhere provided the base of support for the Cuban Revolutionary Party. Courtesy Florida Photographic Collection, The Florida Memory Project, State Archives of Florida.

Top: Inauguration of the Republic, May 20, 1902. In the former Palace of the Captain General, pictured in center: Tomás Estrada Palma, General Máximo Gómez, and American General Leonard Wood, the outgoing Governor General. Author's Collection.

Bottom: Group of teachers, ca. 1900. Teaching was one of the few careers open to Cuban women. As women entered the workforce in increasing numbers during the First Republic, they organized a suffrage party and feminist clubs to press their political rights. Author's Collection.

Top: Plantation Rosario at Aguacate, Cuba, 1904. United States investors gained control of the Cuban sugar industry in the late nineteenth century, bringing in modern technology to establish huge refineries known as *centrales*. Courtesy Library of Congress, LC-USZ62-97352.

Bottom: F. Rafael Lubian, one of the anti-Batista officers in the *Hotel Nacional* who was wounded in the fighting of October 2, 1933. The defeat of the officers cleared the way for Batista to take full control of the army and then the government. Author's Collection.

Top: Fulgencio Batista, Cuban strongman. Leader of the Sergeant's Revolt of 1933, he rose to command the Cuban army, won election to the presidency in 1940, and returned to power by a military coup in 1952. Author's Collection.

Bottom: President Ramón Grau San Martín and President-elect Carolos Prío Socarrás, celebrating the Auténtico victory in the Presidential Palace, 1948. Courtesy of the Cuban Heritage Collection, University of Miami Libraries, Coral Gables, Florida.

Top: The Tropicana, Havana, 1950s. Regarded as the most beautiful nightclub of its time, its lavish shows were the main attraction for American tourists in the 1940s and 1950s. Author's Collection.

Bottom: Eduardo Chibás, founder and leader of the *Ortodoxo* party, campaigning in Havana. His suicide in 1951 removed the most popular candidate for presidency in 1952. Author's Collection.

Camilo Cienfuegos takes Camp Colómbia, January 1959. The man to his right is Roberto Morales Sobrado, a sergeant in the old army who became the personal bodyguard of Camilo. With Camp Colómbia under the control of Camilo, Fidel was clear to enter Havana several days later. Author's Collection.

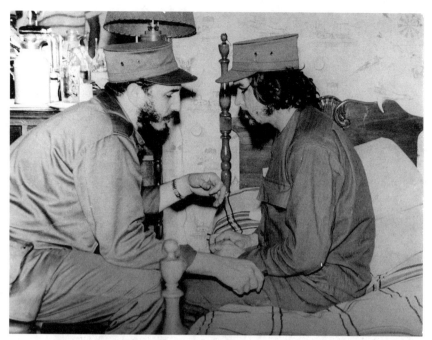

Fidel and Che Guevara, 1959, probably at La Cabaña fortress. Che was Castro's most successful military commander and the leading strategist of the guerilla army. After their victory, he served as president of the National Bank and the Minister of Industry before he left Cuba in 1965 to launch guerilla campaigns in the Congo and Bolivia. Author's Collection.

Above: Fidel Castro arrives in Washington, D.C., April 15, 1959. Castro's first visit to the United States as the leader of the revolutionary government was not well received by officials in Washington. President Eisenhower was conveniently out of town. Vice President Nixon, after a brief meeting with Castro, concluded that he represented a threat to the United States. Courtesy Library of Congress, LC-U9-2315-6.

Opposite top: Vílma Espín, speaking at the tenth anniversary of the Cuban Federation of Women, Havana, August 23, 1970. Wife of Raúl Castro, President of the Cuban Federation of Women, and a member of the Central Committee of the Communist party, Espín was one of the most powerful women in the revolutionary government. Author's Collection.

Opposite bottom: ¡Viva Cuba Libre! Central Havana, June 2002. Free Cuba! remains a popular slogan in Havana and Miami. Author's Collection.

Tourists in Old Havana, 1991. To recover from the economic crisis caused
by the collapse of the Soviet Union, the Cuban government promoted
tourism. European companies invested in hotels and resorts in Havana and
Varadero beach, bringing in hundreds of thousands of tourists in the
1990s. Author's Collection.

CHAPTER FOUR

The Second Republic, 🌿 1934–1958 🌿

*E*very Sunday, Eduardo Chibás would go on the radio and denounce the government, firing away at some corrupt or inept official. Chibás, founder and leader of the *Partido del Pueblo Cubano* (PPC, Cuban People's Party, known as the *Ortodoxos*) was the most popular political entertainer around. This fascinating and unpredictable politician delighted the masses by defending his honor in the old-fashioned method, using sabers and pistols as well as rhetoric in his modern crusade to cleanse the political system. "Crazy Eddie," as he was known, had broken with President Carlos Prío Socarrás, leader of the *Partido Revolucionario Cubano-Auténtico* (PRC-A, Cuban Revolutionary Party, known as the *Auténticos*) because widespread corruption in government dishonored the memory of José Martí, which it claimed to represent. By 1951, Chibás and the Ortodoxos were engaged in a political brawl with Prío and the Auténticos for the right to carry on the revolutionary program of Martí.

On August 5, 1951, Chibás was expected to present evidence to support his charges against Aureliano Sánchez Arango, minister of education and his likely competitor in the upcoming presidential election. However, Crazy Eddie simply repeated his allegation that Sánchez Arango had stolen money allocated for student lunches, with no evidence to back up his charge. He concluded his broadcast with an unusually exuberant call to arms: "Forward! People of Cuba, goodbye! This is my last call!" Chibás then pulled out a gun and shot himself in the abdomen. Unfortunately for him, he did not know that his broadcast had ended. His listeners did not hear what he intended to be his last and most dramatic gesture, a suicide on public radio. Chibás died eleven days later.

63

Crazy Eddie sacrificed himself for the country, becoming another notable name on a long list of patriots and martyrs that included Hatuey, Plácido, and Martí. The suicide of Eduardo Chibás saddened but hardly surprised a people accustomed to martyrdom as an end to a life dedicated to the cause. Chibás and the generation of 1930, like Martí and the generation of 1895 before it, had failed to create the ideal republic through the redemptive revolution that had been promised in the 1890s. The revolutionary ideals of 1933 had been reversed by a military coup in January 1934, buried under a series of corrupt administrations, and forgotten in a morass of political gang warfare that engulfed Cuba in the 1940s. Historian Jaime Suchlicki speculates that Chibás felt that "his death might produce what his life had not—the revolution Martí had envisioned." Many others would risk their lives in a desperate struggle for Cuba Libre in the 1950s, including a young disciple of Eddie Chibás named Fidel Castro.

THE POLITICS OF THE SECOND REPUBLIC, 1934–1952

The nationalist and reformist impulses that had generated the revolution of 1933, however, did not end with Batista's 1934 coup. Fulgencio Batista y Zaldivar, born in 1901 to poor mulatto parents in Oriente Province, personally represented a middle-class intrusion of color into the political system. He did not *own* a sugar plantation like former President Menocal; he *cut* sugar cane as a boy. He joined the army in 1921, rose to the rank of sergeant, and became a stenographer. Known as the pretty mulatto, his personal charm and sharp intellect gave him some strength within the army when the revolution of 1933 erupted.

Batista ruled Cuba with a mixture of reform and repression as the power behind the throne or on it between 1934 and 1944. He imposed martial law, shut down the university, outlawed all unions, and repressed more than one hundred strikes in 1934 and 1935. Antonio Guiteras refused to collaborate with Batista and organized a rebel group known as *Joven Cuba* (Young Cuba) to fight in the countryside. By March 1935, political disorder threatened to sweep a new revolutionary government into power. But Batista cracked down even harder, sending opponents to prison, exile, or the firing squad. In May, army units cornered Guiteras in Matanzas and killed him. Following the death of the most energetic and dedicated leader of the revolution of 1933, a relative political calm settled over the island.

With Batista in power the United States did not need the Platt Amendment because he provided the order and stability demanded by foreign investors and the Cuban elite. After crushing his opponents, he co-opted them, beginning with the Communists in 1937. Batista legalized the Communist party and allowed it to operate openly; in return, the party pledged to support him. He also announced a three-year reform program that included workers' health insurance, consumer cooperatives, and a limited agrarian reform. He sponsored a rural education program that provided the first formal schooling to more than 100,000 people.

Batista's most important contribution to the new republic, however, was undoubtedly the Constitution of 1940. He allowed Grau and other opponents, including Eduardo Chibás and Carlos Prío Socarrás, to serve in a constitutional convention to draft a new charter for Cuba. The result of this unprecedented example of political cooperation was a liberal document that empowered the state to expropriate property, implement an agrarian reform, and promote social welfare. The constitution gave women the right to vote and guaranteed basic civil liberties to all Cubans. It guaranteed workers an eight-hour day, a minimum wage, and the right to collective bargaining. The Constitution of 1940 reflected the reformist and nationalist ideals of the generation of 1930. However, as historian Ramon Eduardo Ruíz notes, "instead of legislating the revolution into existence, it marked its culmination."

Batista was elected president in a free and fair election and inaugurated on October 10, 1940. His greatest accomplishment during his four years as constitutional president was having laid the foundation for a democratic political system. With the sugar industry booming due to the elimination of Cuba's Asian competitors during World War II, Batista gave democracy a chance to take root. He allowed the opposition, led by Grau and the Auténticos, to participate in politics and criticize his government. Moreover, he respected the Constitutional prohibition against reelection, presided over a fair election, and transferred power to Grau in 1944.

Grau's victory in 1944 was hailed by many as a triumph and vindication of the revolutionaries of 1933. But Grau had lost the energy and ambition that once drove him into power. Both Grau and his successor, Carlos Prío, succumbed to the temptations of office, squandering their one and only opportunity to provide Cuba with an honest government that would implement the progressive provisions of the Constitution of 1940. Public cynicism grew worse during eight years of Auténtico rule (1944–52). According to historian Louis Perez, "embezzlement, graft, corruption, and malfeasance of public office permeated every branch of national, provincial, and municipal government. The public trust was transformed into a private till."

With foreign investors controlling the commanding heights of the Cuban economy, the public sector represented one of the few lucrative careers open to Cubans. Grau and Prío rewarded their loyalists with positions in the government, from which they could extort and embezzle money. The number of civil servants exploded from 60,000 in 1943 to 186,000 in 1950. Salaries of these public officials accounted for 80 percent of the 1949–50 national budget, leaving little revenue to fund social and economic programs. Government service remained a lucrative opportunity for personal enrichment, a sad trend that had characterized the old republic that they had destroyed in 1933. When Grau left office in 1948, he was accused of embezzling an astounding $174 million!

As corruption sullied the good name of the Auténticos, Eduardo Chibás led a faction of idealists out of the party to form the Ortodoxo party in May 1947. The Ortodoxos claimed to represent the true ideals of José Martí and the legacy of the Generation of 1930. Over the next four years, as a senator and leader of the Ortodoxos, Chibás raged against the corrupt practices of his former allies. His slogan, "honor against wealth," appealed to a public increasingly skeptical of its political leaders, all of whom apparently had no shame when it came to corruption and using violence to defend it.

Grau and Prío encouraged organized political violence by funding it and protecting its young leaders, the "boys," as Grau called them. Three main political gangs operated during the Auténtico years: *Acción Revolucionaria Guiteras* (ARG, Guiteras Revolutionary Action), led by Fabio Ruíz; *Movimiento Socialista Revolucionario* (MSR, Revolutionary Socialist Movement), directed by former Communist party member Rolando Masferrer; and the *Unión Insurreccional Revolucionario* (UIR, Revolutionary Insurrectional Union), run by Emilio Tró. These organizations operated like organized criminal networks affiliated with the government. Grau appointed Mario Salabarría of the MSR to a high post in the National Police. He appointed Emilio Tró of the UIR director of the National Police Academy. The attempt to placate both political gangs through an even distribution of the political spoils served only to incite violence. On September 15, 1947, Major Salabarría attempted to arrest Major Tró for murder. Tró resisted arrest, and a spectacular gunfight ensued for three hours on the streets of Orfila, a neighborhood of Marianao. While the battle raged, cameramen captured gangsterism live, showing the murder of Tró after he had surrendered.

The Orfila shootout was only the most dramatic example of political gangsterism at work. Gunfights on the steps of the capitol and drive-by shootings became commonplace. The gunfighters, many of them not even enrolled in classes, found refuge at the University of Havana, which was supposedly off-limits to the national police. Armed men roamed the campus at will. According to Cuban historian Jaime Suchlicki, the political warfare at the University of Havana "was only a microcosm of Cuba's political life. An entire system of nepotism, favoritism, and gangsterism predominated."

This environment shaped the political development of a law student named Fidel Castro. By the time Castro enrolled in the university in 1945, it was already a political battleground. He was born in Banes in 1928, the son of a Spanish colono who cultivated sugar cane near the United Fruit Company plantations. Nominally interested in pursuing a law degree, Castro displayed greater interest in national politics. Although he criticized gangsterism, the MSR tagged him as a UIR man. At one point Major Salabarría threatened to kill Castro if he did not cease his verbal assaults on gangsterism and corruption. Fidel did not back down, but from that time on he carried a pistol with him.

By 1947 Castro had become a recognized figure in campus politics, known for his fiery public attacks against political violence and corruption, prominent themes in the speeches of his idol, Crazy Eddie. Castro attended the inaugural meeting of the Ortodoxo party and subsequently organized the Radical Action group within the party. Unlike many of the other gang leaders, who apparently found violence a satisfactory end in itself, Castro sought national redemption through revolutionary action, in the tradition of Guiteras. As a member of the Ortodoxo party, however, he campaigned hard for Chibás in 1948 and initially sought political change through electoral means.

In the 1952 elections, Castro campaigned for a seat in the Chamber of Deputies as a member of the Ortodoxo party. His campaign was cut short on March 10, 1952, when Batista deposed President Prío in a quick and relatively bloodless coup. He cancelled the elections (in which polls had indicated that he would finish third) and installed himself as president. Batista had violated the same Constitution of 1940 that he had enacted, but few Cubans mourned the death of the Auténtico government. Some people even held out some hope that Batista would put an end to graft, corruption, scandals, and violence. As it happened, the coup of 1952 unleashed a political firestorm that engulfed the island within seven years.

THE BATISTATO, 1952–1958

"The people and I are dictators," Fulgencio Batista explained. Although he professed loyalty to the Constitution of 1940, he suspended civil liberties, shut down congress, postponed the presidential elections, and suspended all political parties. The former reformist who had forged an alliance with the

Communists was now an anti-Communist, playing to the Cold War mentality then prevailing in Washington. He ruled with an iron fist, re-establishing the order and stability that the United States demanded of Cuba. Batista's repression targeted all those who disturbed the peace, including the political gangs. Without the Auténticos to protect the political groups, the gangsters had to adapt to the new reality or fight against it. Rolando Masferrer and the MSR decided to collaborate with Batista and became a private army in defense of the *Batistato*.

The military challenge to Batista's dictatorship was not long in coming. On the morning of July 26, 1953, Fidel Castro led nearly one hundred rebels in a suicidal attack on the Moncada army garrison in Santiago, which was defended by one thousand troops. After a furious one-hour gunfight, Castro withdrew and ran toward the Sierra Maestra, where he hoped to reorganize his rebel army. Batista's army responded with a brutality rarely seen in previous rebellions, hunting down, torturing, and executing sixty-eight rebels. Abel Santamaría, the second in command of the operation, was captured in a nearby hospital and tortured to death. Luckily for Castro, he was captured and taken to the Santiago prison rather than the Moncada garrison, where he surely would have been murdered. Castro turned this devastating defeat into triumph at his subsequent trial, in which he concluded his self-defense with the memorable phrase: "Condemn me, it does not matter. History will absolve me." The tribunal nevertheless sentenced Castro to fifteen years in prison at the Isle of Pines.

At the time, Batista did not take Castro and his rebel group seriously. He rescheduled the presidential elections for November 1954, but he did not intend to lose them. Former president Ramón Grau discredited himself by attempting a comeback through these elections, even though he pulled out of the campaign when it became obvious that Batista would control the outcome. On November 1, 1954, Batista was elected president for a four-year term without opposition. With only 40 percent of the eligible voters casting a ballot, Batista could not possibly claim that he had triumphed in a democratic and constitutional election.

The traditional political opposition demanded a return to the constitutional order. In early 1956, Batista entered into negotiations with representatives of the Auténticos and the Ortodoxos in a Civic Dialogue designed to restore a semblance of civility and stability to the government. The opposition demanded new presidential elections in 1956, but Batista would not concede any point. He refused to cut short his term and insisted that the presidential election would take place as scheduled, in November 1958. There would be no political compromise. The Civic Dialogue collapsed, and with it the last chance for a peaceful return to the constitutional order.

With the regime firmly established, Batista attempted to modernize and diversify the economy. Sugar production had recovered from the low levels of the Depression years, but the economy still suffered from over-dependence on a single export crop. Since 1934, sugar exports to the United States had been regulated by a quota system administered by the U.S. Department of Agriculture, which assigned a percentage of the market to foreign and domestic producers. Cuba's share of the American market subsequently increased from 25.4 percent in 1933 to 31.4 percent in 1937, stimulating an increase in production as well, from 1.9 million tons in 1933 to 2.9 million tons in 1938. Cuban sugar production continued to increase to 5.8 million tons in 1948 as Cuba established itself as the world's largest producer of sugar. With sugar exports constituting 80 to 90 percent of Cuba's total exports, Cuba's economic development hinged on the decisions made by the United States government.

Cuban reformers had been promoting economic diversification against the opposition of the powerful sugar lobby for years. In the 1950s, the booms caused by World War II and the Korean War ended, leaving the Cuban economy stagnant. The Gross National Product (GNP) grew only 1 percent in the period 1950 to 1958. To increase production and raise the standard of living, other agricultural and industrial products would have to lead the way because sugar production had reached its peak. The World Bank estimated that Cuba would have to harvest a record 9 million tons just to increase the GNP growth rate to 2 percent. But even if the Cubans managed to produce such a record crop, there was no guarantee that the United States would buy all of it. The Cuban sugar industry simply could not drive the economic development required to raise the general standard of living. According to historian Lou Perez, "sugar had ceased to be a source of economic growth and could not sustain continued economic development."

The fundamental problem in Cuba, the World Bank noted, was not that there was too much sugar; the problem was that Cuba did not produce much of anything else. Over-reliance on sugar exports to the United States had obstructed economic diversification projects since the 1920s. A new reciprocity treaty in 1934 actually worked against Cuba's 1927 Customs Tariff Law, designed to spur industrialization and economic diversification. The Reciprocity Treaty of 1934 granted American manufactured goods tax-free entry into Cuba, thereby discouraging the development of Cuban industry. With Cuba importing 75 percent of its manufactured goods from the United States, there was little chance that Cuban industrialists could compete with American enterprises. The Cuban economy was double locked in a state of dependency, relying excessively on exports of one crop to one market and imports of manufactured goods from the same market.

Cuban industrialists lobbied for economic diversification against stiff opposition from sugar producers, who fought hard to defend their share of the American market. *Hacendados* (mill owners) and *colonos* (cane growers) feared that any protective tariffs for Cuban industry would result in a reduction in the U.S. sugar quota. The industrialists nevertheless presented a powerful case for reform. In 1946, the National Association of Industrialists explained: "In order to obtain our economic independence, it is imperative that we carry out an integral reform of our economic system, which is a colonial one, based on producing raw materials which we sell in only one market at a price and conditions imposed by the buyer."

With the Cuban economy stagnant, Batista had no choice but to pursue economic diversification. In 1955 the government issued a National Program for Economic Action that called for an end to Cuban dependency. "Cuba cannot continue to depend almost exclusively on sugar to sustain its population, nor wait for solutions through preferential treatment from the United States. . . . If we do not structure and orient our economy to secure a just and adequate standard of living for our people, unfortunate days await us."

To promote diversification Batista turned to a familiar friend: North American capital. The value of American investment had dropped to $686 million in 1953. To attract more foreign investment, Batista offered a package of incentives that included guarantees against nationalization, lenient regulations, and tax concessions. American investors poured money into mining, manufacturing, ranching, and utilities. The King Ranch of Texas invested $5.7 million to develop a 40,000-acre cattle ranch in Camagüey Province; Standard Oil modernized its petroleum refinery outside Havana; W. R. Grace acquired a paper-container firm; U.S. Rubber initiated construction of a $5 million plant; the Freeport Sulfur Company won a concession to build a $75 million plant at Moa Bay; and the United States government invested $40 million to increase production at its nickel plant in Oriente Province. In 1958, the estimated value of American direct investment in Cuba had increased to $1 billion.

American capital was no longer concentrated in the sugar industry. The most valuable enterprise on the island was the Cuban Electric Company, a subsidiary of Electric Bond and Share of New York, with a book value in excess of $256 million. This company's poor service and illicit ties to Batista made it a popular symbol of foreign exploitation and corruption. The Cuban Telephone Company, a subsidiary of International Telephone and Telegraph, was equally unpopular. By attracting foreign investment outside agriculture, Batista initiated a type of diversification that would change the form but not the substance of Cuba's dependence on the United States. The economy was growing stronger and more diverse, but it still depended on trade and investment with the United States.

Batista also attempted to diversify the economy by promoting tourism, the most conspicuous and controversial aspect of his development program. American tourists had made the island a favorite travel destination in the 1920s, but the great boom in hotel and casino development began during the Batistato. When Batista took power in 1952, the only successful casinos operated at the Tropicana, Montmarte, and Sans Souci nightclubs. Batista issued a law that permitted gambling in all Havana hotels valued at more than $1 million. The government charged casino operators $25,000 for a gambling license and a $2,000 monthly fee, plus 20 percent of the profits, paid on a quarterly basis. These were only the official fees. Lower-ranking public officials, including policemen, also took a cut in the casino business, which became a sensational and bittersweet success of the Batistato.

Between 1952 and 1958, twenty-eight new hotel casinos opened in and around Havana. In the Vedado district alone, three modern high-rises went up, the Habana Riviera (1957), the Capri (1957), and the Habana Hilton (1958). These new hotels competed with a refurbished *Hotel Nacional*, the pride of Havana since the 1930s. Few, however, could compare with the Riviera, the crown jewel in the illicit empire of Meyer Lansky, business associate of Batista and mobster Lucky Luciano. Lansky put up most of the $14 to $18 million in construction costs for the 21-story, 374-room Riviera, with Batista kicking in $6 million in government money. Lansky's hotel became a landmark on the Malecón, Havana's seafront boulevard, and a symbol of Cuba in the 1950s. For the grand opening of the Riviera on December 10, 1957, Lansky brought in Ginger Rogers from Hollywood.

By 1958, Cuba was attracting 300,000 tourists per year. They could sip a daiquiri at the Floridita Bar—where a reserved table always awaited part-time Havana resident Ernest Hemingway—or a mojito at La Bodeguita del Medio—a bohemian bar and restaurant described by actor Erroll Flynn as the "best place to get drunk." At night they could take in a floor show at the Hotel Nacional and gamble in the Riviera's casino. They could hire prostitutes and buy drugs on the street. Everything was seemingly encouraged; nothing was prohibited. To partake of this wide-open island fantasy, one only had to drive onto a ferry in Key West or hop onto the "Gambler's Special," a Pan American flight that departed Miami every Thursday night.

Few tourists knew or cared that Meyer Lansky, the undisputed king of the Havana crime syndicate, ran the casinos at the Hotel Nacional, Riviera, and Montmarte nightclub. Santo Traficante, Jr., who had run the numbers racket in Tampa, Florida, ran the Sans Souci casino and reportedly had a cut in the Havana Hilton and Capri. Lefty Clark, another underworld figure known to the FBI, managed the casino at the Tropicana, regarded as the "most beautiful nightclub in the world." "Havana was transformed into a center of commercialized vice of all sorts, underwritten by organized crime from the United States and protected by Batista's police officials," historian Lou Perez explains.

AMERICANIZATION AND CUBANIDAD

The infusion of American tourists and the Mafia added a new dimension to the struggle to define Cubanidad, the Cuban national character. Now, American tourists and the Cubans who catered to them were redefining Cubanidad to satisfy a foreign audience. Cuban politicians, businesspeople, writers, artists, and athletes had been asserting their national identity for decades, and foreign influences had always influenced the national discourse on Cubanidad. However, as the political struggles against Batista intensified in the 1950s, the cultural conflict over identify became part of the national struggle against dictatorship and foreign domination.

Havana reflected and exposed the paradox that Cuba had become. The population of Cuba had quadrupled since 1899, reaching 5.8 million in 1953. Havana was now a sprawling metropolis of 1 million residents, with the most affluent people living in the exclusive neighborhood of Miramar, west of Havana. The magnificent mansions that lined Fifth Avenue surpassed the old aristocrats' homes in Vedado and rivaled the estates in New York or Paris. With a central promenade featuring spacious parks and fountains, Fifth Avenue was indeed the haven of a new Cuban and foreign elite. They lived on or near "the" Fifth Avenue and played in their exclusive social clubs, the most aristocratic of all was the Habana Yacht Club, with an oceanfront clubhouse open only to members with acceptable family credentials. Even Fulgencio Batista, the poor mulatto from Oriente Province, was denied admission to the yacht club; he had to join the slightly less exclusive Biltmore Yacht and Country Club. For those who circulated in the plush residences, hotels, and countryclubs of Vedado and Miramar, Havana was a resplendent capital city, with convenient airline connections to Miami and New York, to which the Havana elite generally looked for cultural inspiration.

But there was another Havana, one not frequented by the American tourists. In the slums of Luyano or across the bay in Regla, a predominantly Afro-Cuban community, Cubans lived in a world far removed from the splendor of Miramar. In these poorer neighborhoods, where there was ample evidence that Cuba's sugar-based economy had failed to spread prosperity equitably, the expressions of Cuban culture reflected more African than American influences. Although Cubans boasted an average per capita income of $374, the second highest in Latin America, few members of the urban poor had the opportunity to travel or shop abroad. The Cubans who lived in Vedado and Miramar were increasingly tied to and benefited from the material culture of the United States, but the Cubans who lived outside these exclusive neighborhoods remained tied to and increasingly protective of a more traditional Cuba that was increasingly hostile to the emerging society and culture of the upper classes in Havana.

The glitz and glamour of Havana contrasted even more sharply with the grim material realities of the rural poor. Approximately 25 percent of the total labor force worked in the sugar industry. The typical agricultural worker earned less than $80 per month, and due to the seasonal nature of the sugar industry, nearly 60 percent of all Cuban workers were either unemployed or underemployed. They had little to no access to health care or education, and they had few nonviolent outlets for their political grievances. Although nearly 1.5 million Cubans belonged to a labor union in 1958, the *Confederación de Trabajadores Cubanos* (CTC, Cuban Workers Confederation) had been completely co-opted by the government. Eusebio Mujal, secretary general of the CTC, became associated with the corruption and repression of the Batistato. The state protected the laborers in return for their political support, but it would not allow the unions to press for higher wages or better working conditions through strikes or political demonstrations. The result was that the progressive labor legislation that Batista sponsored in the 1930s produced few tangible benefits for either urban or rural workers in the 1950s.

Social justice was still only a dream for Cuban workers, particularly those living in rural areas. American tourists did not have to go far outside of Havana to see evidence of poverty. American Ambassador Arthur Gardner wrote: "It is hard for a person who comes to Cuba and sees so many signs of building and prosperity to realize that only a few miles back from the city hundreds of thousands of people have only the bare necessities of life. Until this sore has been healed by the opportunity to work, Cuba will remain in a restless stage."

Nonetheless, most Americans' perceptions of Cubans derived from their interactions with the people who served and entertained them in Havana's hotels, casinos, bars, and brothels, not the Afro-Cuban communities of Regla nor even the urban middle classes of Santiago. Cuban culture as it existed in Havana became increasingly popular in the United States, giving the average American an opportunity to know a slice of Cuban culture through music and dance. Between the 1930s and 1950s, a succession of Cuban dance crazes hit the American market: the rumba, conga, cha-cha-chá, and mambo. Xavier Cugat, Dámaso Pérez Prado, and Desi Arnaz played Americanized versions of these Cuban rhythms and the American people went crazy. The most popular symbol of Cuban culture came to be the Ricky Ricardo character on the *I Love Lucy* television show. Played by Desi Arnaz, real-life husband of comedienne Lucille Ball, Ricky and Lucy created one of the most watched television programs in history. The show propagated a stereotypical version of Cuban culture. Louis Perez argues that the Ricky Ricardo character "easily reinforced the dominant images: rumba band leader, heavily accented English, excitable, always seeming to be slightly out of place and hence slightly vulnerable, perhaps even childlike and non-threatening."

Americans were beginning to love an image of Cuba that was increasingly unlike Cuba. They adored a version of Cuba that they helped to create, a vision popularized by the grand casinos of Havana, the gaudy floor shows of the Tropicana, or *I Love Lucy.* Havana was not like the rest of Cuba, and not all Cuban men were handsome band leaders married to a wacky American redhead. American cultural influences shaped but did not dictate Cuban discourse on cultural identity. The fact that Americans seemingly adored the light-skinned Ricky Ricardo did not mean that Cubans regarded him more highly than the dark-skinned Celia Cruz, born in the poor Santo Suarez neighborhood of Havana in the mid-1920s. In 1950 she became the lead vocalist for the famous group *La Sonora Matancera* and recorded dozens of albums on her way to becoming the "Queen of Salsa." Unlike other singers, she refused to record in English even though she toured the United States in the 1950s. Perhaps the best popular Cuban musicians never sought nor received validation in the American market. The singer, composer, and band leader Benny Moré contributed some of the most memorable *mambo* songs ever recorded, but this self-trained musician never starred in his own television show. Nevertheless, Celia Cruz and Benny Moré, two of the greatest stars in Cuba's distinguished musical history, were widely adored by the Cuban people and their music was more authentically Cuban than that shaped by American musical tastes.

Cuban writers, poets, and artists, such as Alejo Carpentier, Nicolás Guillén, and Wilfredo Lam, continued to express uniquely Cuban identities in the form and content of their works. Carpentier, one of the best Latin American novelists of all time, expressed the current strains of surrealism in novels such as *The Kingdom of this World* and *The Lost Steps*. Guillén, a mulatto, infused his poetry with Afro-Cuban rhythms and demonstrated the vibrant existence of a true mulatto culture in Cuba. A member of the Communist Party of Cuba, Guillén did not become Cuba's national poet by mimicking American styles. Wilfredo Lam, the Cuban-born son of a Chinese immigrant and an Afro-Cuban mother, circulated in the most prestigious art academies of Cuba, Spain, and France and counted Pablo Picasso as a personal friend. Lam's evocative paintings, a mixture of expressionism and surrealism, were in no way derivative of American art.

Elements of Cuban life and culture mixed freely with and prospered as a result of contact with North American currents. Cuban baseball, for example, flourished in the 1950s and many players, such as Orestes "Minnie" Miñoso played for professional teams in the United States. Cuban baseball fans followed the World Series intently and knew enough about the New York Yankees and the Brooklyn Dodgers to fight about them. Cuban fans, however, rooted with equal passion for their teams, including the Havana Lions, the Marianao Tigers, the Almendares Blues, and the Cienfuegos Elephants. Cubans occasionally expressed their nationalism through their love of baseball. In 1953, one journalist argued that the Almendares Blues could have "whaled the tar out of such teams as the Pittsburgh Pirates."

Although American tourists, businesspeople, and gangsters permeated aspects of popular Cuban culture, particularly in Havana, Americanization did not sweep away the sense of Cubanidad that artists and intellectuals had begun to articulate in the 1920s. Various strains of Cuban nationalism existed, often in opposition to each other. A modern form in Havana and the developing beach resort of Varadero manifested strong American influences, but a traditional form drew strength from deep Cuban roots and defined itself partly out of opposition to American influence. Cuba's cultural leaders, many of them persons of African descent, added a powerful cultural component to the long-standing political opposition to foreign domination, a tradition that had defined Cuban nationalism since the late nineteenth century. The American tourists and investors who enjoyed and profited from the American boom in the 1950s could hardly recognize a latent anti-Americanism taking root among the Cuban people. Americans stereotyped Cubans as friendly, fun-loving, emotional, and volatile, prone to rebellion in politics but hardly a threat to American interests. Thus, few American businesspeople or diplomats paid much attention to political violence like the assault on the Moncada barracks. Fewer Americans could believe that a former political gangster like Fidel Castro could overthrow Batista and initiate a truly radical revolutionary program.

THE INSURRECTION

After Fidel Castro was released from prison in a general amnesty of May 1955, he refused to renounce his right of insurrection. Like so many other opponents of the Batista regime, Castro recognized that the dictator would not surrender power voluntarily. He had shown no willingness to compromise in the Civic Dialogue of 1956, leaving his political opponents only two alternatives: collaboration with his increasingly corrupt and dictatorial regime, or armed rebellion. The two parties that claimed to represent the true legacy of Martí, the Auténticos and the Ortodoxos showed a decided preference for the former. One of the few political leaders who dared to pursue the more dangerous option was Fidel Castro. Rather than join the Communists, a revolutionary organization that would not fight, Fidel formed one that would, the *Movimiento 26 de Julio* (M-26-7, 26th of July Movement). Castro left for Mexico to organize a rebel army on July 7, 1955, proclaiming himself a disciple of José Martí: "the hour has come to take rights and not to beg for them."

Soon after Fidel arrived in Mexico, his brother Raúl introduced him to Ernesto Guevara, a twenty-seven-year-old Argentine doctor who shared Raúl's Marxist inclinations. Guevara had fled Guatemala in dismay after the U.S. Central Intelligence Agency (CIA) orchestrated the overthrow of Jacobo Arbenz's revolutionary government in 1954. Looking for a chance to fight for an "authentic revolution," Guevara was eager to learn more about Castro's revolutionary ambitions. After one fateful night, Castro and Guevara formed a revolutionary partnership. Ernesto saw that Castro had "an unshakable faith that once he left he would arrive in Cuba, that once he arrived he would fight, that once he began fighting he would win." When the meeting broke up at dawn the next day, Ernesto had enlisted as the doctor of Fidel's rebel army.

Fidel and Ernesto shared a determination to fight as well as a total lack of formal military training. Given the poor performance at Moncada, Castro had to develop a viable military strategy if he seriously hoped to overthrow a dictatorship defended by a 40,000-man army trained and supplied by the United States. Castro had enough good sense to hire Alberto Bayo, a Republican veteran of the Spanish Civil War, to train his rebel army in the art of guerrilla warfare. Bayo urged Castro not to fight the Cuban army on its terms. If he did, the rebels would surely lose; if they adopted guerrilla tactics, Bayo assured him, they would eventually win. While Castro concentrated on raising money for his rebel army from sympathizers in the United States and Latin America, Guevara, nicknamed "Che" by his Cuban comrades, listened intently and became Bayo's star pupil. From Bayo, Che Guevara learned how a small, mobile force could defeat a superior enemy by using hit-and-run tactics, fighting on ground of its choosing, and gaining the support of the peasantry by promoting land reform.

Alberto Bayo set up a training camp outside of Mexico City while Castro was still abroad raising funds. He received a large contribution from former president Carlos Prío Socarrás. Meanwhile, the M-26-7 underground in Havana, composed primarily of young middle-class men and women, continued to organize, recruit, and raise money. In the summer of 1956, the Mexican police raided the rebel training camp and set back Castro's plans; now Mexican, American, and Cuban authorities knew of Castro's plans to invade Cuba. In the tradition of José Martí and Antonio Maceo, Castro intended to organize an army in exile, invade eastern Cuba, and spark a nationwide rebellion. No sophisticated surveillance or covert infiltration was required to learn of Castro's plans; before the end of 1956 he publicly boasted of them. The only questions were precisely when and where Castro's rebel force would land.

On November 24, 1956, Castro and eighty-two rebels boarded a fifty-eight-foot yacht called the *Granma* near Veracruz, Mexico. On this pleasure craft designed to hold only twenty-five people, Castro's rebel army sailed through the Yucatan Channel, across the Caribbean, and slid to a stop in a mangrove swamp on December 2, 1956, two days behind schedule. The landing was supposed to coincide with a diversionary strike led by Frank País in Santiago on November 30. País attacked as ordered, but Fidel's main body was still at sea. So when the *Granma* landed in the wrong place at the wrong time, Castro's plans had already gone awry. The rebels disembarked in the swamp and hacked their way to dry land with enemy aircraft and army battalions in pursuit. Three days later, Castro's rebel army was surprised and completely routed at Alegría del Pío. Only sixteen of the eighty-two men who disembarked the *Granma* survived the battle of Alegría del Pío; Batista's army hunted down and killed most of the others.

Yet two years later, the survivors of that disaster marched triumphantly into Havana as liberators, including Che Guevara, Camilo Cienfuegos, and Raúl Castro. The scattered rebels eventually received shelter and assistance from Celia Sánchez Manduley, the 26th of July Movement coordinator in

Manzanillo, who had prepared a network of peasant sympathizers to support the rebel army. Batista declared that Castro had been killed and called off the pursuit of him on December 13. Guillermo García, a peasant recruited by Celia Sánchez, helped Castro and the other survivors to move into the Sierra Maestra, where they reorganized and prepared to launch a guerilla campaign. From the costly mistakes at Moncada and Alegría del Pío, Castro finally learned the value of unconventional warfare. He would never again lose a battle.

On January 17, 1957, Castro attacked and captured a small army outpost at La Plata, on the southern coast of Oriente Province. This time, the rebels surrounded the barracks and attacked under the cover of darkness. After a thirty-minute skirmish, they marched off into the mountains, hoping that the army would send patrols in pursuit. Castro set up an ambush at a place called Arroyo del Infierno and waited for the army to fall into his trap. A platoon led by Lieutenant Sánchez Mosquera marched into the ambush on January 22 and withdrew after a brief gunfight, giving Castro a second minor victory. The skirmishes at La Plata and Arroyo del Infierno, however, established a pattern in the guerrilla campaign that Fidel and Che subsequently utilized with great effect. The rebel units would hit an army position, retreat into the mountains, and dare the army to pursue them. Over the next eighteen months, Castro and Che never again offered the army battle in the open field, knowing that there they lay vulnerable to overwhelming artillery and air power. Instead, they skillfully used their small size and mobility to great advantage over the numerically superior Cuban army, which had no training in counterinsurgency warfare.

Castro's mastery of propaganda proved to be an even more valuable asset than his guerrilla strategy. On February 17, *New York Times* journalist Herbert Matthews interviewed Fidel at a secret location. During the interview, Castro received pre-arranged dispatches from fictitious rebel columns at other camps. At the time, Castro really had no more than thirty rebels under his command, and they hardly controlled the ground on which they stood. Nevertheless, Matthews published the sensational news that Castro's rebel army *controlled* the Sierra Maestra. Castro himself could not have written a more positive article. Matthews set the tone of media coverage for the rest of the insurrection, portraying Castro's rebels as romantic and idealistic young men fighting for a just cause, with Fidel aspiring to restore Cuban democracy.

Castro's army, however, was not alone in the struggle to oust Batista by force of arms. Students at the University of Havana led by José Antonio Echevarría organized a clandestine organization called the *Directorio Revolucionario Estudiantil* (DRE, Revolutionary Student Directorate) to fight the dictatorship as well. Unlike Castro, who fought isolated army outposts in Oriente Province, Echevarría wanted to strike the dictatorship at the top. On the afternoon of March 13, fifty DRE commandos attacked the presidential palace. The students stormed through the gates and a few fought their way up to Batista's office on the second floor, but the dictator had already escaped through a secret passage. The army drove the students out of the palace and hunted them down on the streets, killing Echevarría that same afternoon. Although the DRE failed in its attempt to decapitate the regime, the daring assault established the student organization as one of Batista's most courageous opponents.

The savagery that Batista unleashed against the political opposition further eroded the weak constitutional foundation of his government. On April 20, 1957, the police raided an apartment at Humboldt 7 in Havana, where José Westbrook and three other DRE leaders who had survived the attack were hiding. Westbrook hid in an apartment on a lower floor, but the police recognized him immediately, threw him into the hall, and shot him dead. Another student was machine gunned as he ran down the hall. The other two students jumped out of the window, crashed on the pavement below, and died in a barrage of machine-gun fire while dozens of horrified people looked on.

As Batista grew increasingly corrupt, indifferent, and brutal, he only increased the strength and determination of his adversaries. The regime even began to crumble from within. In April 1956, Colonel Ramón Barquín was arrested for conspiring with other military officers known as *puros*, for their alleged purity and dedication to the Cuban republic. A more significant military rebellion erupted at Cienfuegos naval base on September 5, 1957. There Lieutenant Dionisio Pérez San Román led more than one hundred sailors in revolt, hoping to incite other army and naval units to rise against Batista as well. After some of the most ferocious fighting of the entire insurrection, the Cienfuegos rebels surrendered, not knowing that Batista intended to use them to send a message to all potential conspirators. Lt. San Román was taken to Havana, tortured, and dumped into the sea.

By the beginning of 1958, a full-scale civil war engulfed the island. The ranks of Castro's rebel army swelled with the enlistment of poor peasants from Oriente Province and young volunteers from the cities, allowing Castro to divide the rebel army into independent columns and disperse them throughout the Sierra Maestra. The DRE leadership had been decimated in the aftermath of the assault on the presidential palace, but the students eventually regrouped as a guerrilla force based in the Escambray Mountains of Las Villas province. In Havana, Santiago, and the provincial capitals, young men and women did the dangerous work that kept the guerrillas in the mountains: raising funds, recruiting, buying arms and ammunition, and carrying out raids on selected targets. The repression in Havana grew increasingly barbaric, with mutilated corpses routinely appearing on the streets.

The repression and violence escalated to an intolerable level for the administration of U.S. president Dwight D. Eisenhower. The United States had supported Batista's unconstitutional regime since the March 1952 coup, supplying Batista with the arms and ammunition he needed to keep his army in the field. But on March 14, 1958, the United States suspended all further arms shipments to Batista's government, saying it did not want its arms used in a civil war. Batista found other military suppliers, but the U.S. arms embargo eroded his government's base of political support and reduced the morale of his soldiers. Meanwhile, the CIA secretly supplied limited amounts of funds and equipment to the rebel army, another indication that even the United States favored a change in government.

The decisive military factor was that Batista's army did not know how to fight a counterinsurgency campaign. The army never established a secure cordon around the mountains; it did not engage in search and destroy missions; it rarely used its air power; and it rarely used its superior armaments. Castro slowly won the support of the Oriente peasants by promising them land reform, offering medical assistance, and occasionally attacking or taking money from American-owned sugar companies in eastern Cuba. But as his rebel army rolled up victories, Castro became the most powerful opponent of Batista and the American diplomats and businesspeople who supported him. The longer Castro held out against the regime, the more popular he became, which meant that more recruits, supplies, and intelligence flowed into his rebel camps.

The heaviest fighting of the war occurred in the summer of 1958, when Batista finally mobilized 14,000 troops for a coordinated military offensive. The army drove into rebel territory from the north and the south, hoping to trap the rebels in a deadly pincers movement or drive them onto the plains, where the army would bring in tanks, bombers, and artillery to destroy them. But the rebel defenses prepared by Che Guevara worked as designed. Only three hundred rebels held out against the vastly bigger army, repulsing every attempt to drive them out of their defensive positions. The poor morale and training of the army troops—many of them peasants drafted into service— accounted for the dismal performance of Batista's army. They faced a seasoned and disciplined guerrilla army, familiar with the terrain and the tactics of their enemy. The army offensive stalled in early August. Batista never led his army in the field, preferring to issue orders from his estate outside Havana.

Castro launched a bold counteroffensive in late August 1958. He ordered the columns of Che Guevara and Camilo Cienfuegos to break out of Oriente Province, march across the island, and take the war to central Cuba. If successful, Guevara and Cienfuegos would cut the island in two by preventing Batista from sending supplies and reinforcements to Oriente Province. The two columns left in late August and arrived in Las Villas Province in October, creating a popular sensation along the way. Castro's bearded rebels, sexy and macho young men known as *barbudos*, fired the imagination of all those men and women who still thought it possible to reform a corrupt political system. The handsome Che Guevara, with his trademark black beret, played the role of a foreign redeemer, much like the Dominican General Máximo Gómez in the 1890s. Young men and women took to the streets to fight with the barbudos, not thinking far beyond their immediate desire to destroy the hated Batista regime.

Worse for Batista, his army showed little desire to fight. As Che slowly closed a noose around Santa Clara, taking garrisons one by one, the army often surrendered as soon as Che showed up. While Fidel and several hundred guerrillas kept the pressure on in Santiago Province, the province of Las Villas became the decisive battleground of the insurrection. In late December, with Che's guerrillas coordinating their attacks with the DRE to take Santa Clara, Batista sent reinforcements and supplies to the besieged city in an armored train. Che anticipated the attempt and arrayed his forces to derail it. On December 29, the rebel forces captured the armored train along with nearly four hundred soldiers and hundreds of wooden crates filled with arms, ammunition, and supplies. With the train went Batista's last hope for survival.

The battle raged on in Santa Clara, with people picking up arms and following the rebels into the center of town, where the last resistance held out. Fidel Castro's guerrilla army by this time led a broadly based popular insurrection fighting by conventional methods in virtually every city and town in each of Cuba's six provinces. The *Granma* invasion, followed by two years of guerrilla warfare, had finally sparked a general insurrection of a diverse political coalition—united only in its determination to overthrow an unconstitutional regime. Not many people had given much thought to the political program of Fidel Castro, who repeatedly insisted that his main objective was the restoration of the Constitution of 1940. He promised to redeem the vision of Cuba Libre and expressly denied allegations that he was a communist. There was little reason for the public to believe otherwise. The Communist Party had, in fact, condemned Castro's revolutionary movement, although in the summer of 1958 it began to collaborate with the M-26-7, particularly Che, the most radical intellectual of the organization.

Still, there was no general consensus on a political program that would unite all the diverse factions in a post-Batista government. Political leaders of the discredited traditional parties, the Auténticos and the Ortodoxos, hoped to restore the political order as it was prior to 1952, a hope not likely to fire the popular imagination as much as the revolutionary pretensions of the barbudos. Some military officers plotted to remove Batista and install a non-communist provisional government that Castro would not dominate. The general public, however, recognized Castro as the uncontested leader of the revolutionary movement, although nobody knew exactly what he intended to do. Batista had not yet deployed his strongest army units against Castro, but by the end of 1958, he recognized that he could not impose a military solution. Batista, knowing that his regime had crumbled underneath him, flew into exile in the Dominican Republic in the predawn hours of January 1, 1959.

A day later, Castro addressed a boisterous crowd in Santiago's Céspedes Park. In a display of raw political power, he named Manuel Urrutia the provisional president, blocking any efforts by his political rivals in Havana to form a reformist government supported by the United States. Cubans and Americans had seen revolutionaries come and go for the previous sixty years, but with a revolutionary army behind him, Castro would tolerate no attempts to frustrate his political ambitions. "This time, luckily for Cuba, the Revolution will truly come into power," Castro explained. "It will not be like 1898, when the North Americans came and made themselves masters of our country. . . . The Revolution will not be made in two days, but now I am sure that for the first time the republic will really be entirely free and the people will have what they deserve."

CHAPTER FIVE

The Revolution,
🌿 1959–1970 🌿

*A*s dawn broke over Havana on January 1, 1959, the streets were empty and relatively quiet. Neither the newspapers nor radio broadcasts contained news of any political developments for Cubans to discuss over their *café con leche*. Gradually, rumors of Batista's resignation and departure spread by word of mouth with a simple message—"*¡Se fue!*"—he left. By noon the rumor had been confirmed and people took to the streets to celebrate, jubilantly singing the national anthem and flying the banner of the 26th of July Movement. Later in the day, some people vented their pent-up frustrations by breaking into the casinos, burning slot machines, and sacking the homes of a few *batistianos*.

Political power in Havana rested momentarily with General Eulogio Cantillo, now chief of staff of a quickly disintegrating army. He wisely handed power to Colonel Ramón Barquín, the anti-Batista officer recently freed from prison, who subsequently arrested General Cantillo, who had allowed Batista to escape. Everyone, including Barquín, already knew that the real power rested in Santiago with Fidel, who had ordered the columns of Che Guevara and Camilo Cienfuegos to march on Havana. Guevara and Camilo took command of La Cabaña and Camp Colombia garrisons without a fight on January 2, while Castro began a triumphal procession across the island, apparently gathering *fidelistas* along the way. The cheering crowds that greeted Castro in every town he passed through created the impression that Castro alone had defeated Batista and that he alone would now decide Cuba's political future. By the time Castro's caravan arrived at the presidential palace on January 8, the rebel army controlled Havana. Castro held only the title of Commander in Chief, but he, not the president he designated—Judge Manuel Urrutia—controlled Cuba's destiny.

Castro spoke briefly to thousands from the balcony of the presidential palace then asked them to clear a path so that he could walk across the plaza to the Malecón. Without a single soldier protecting him, Castro walked unmolested through the crowd. Then he jumped into a jeep and drove along the waterfront through Vedado and on to Camp Colómbia, with thousands cheering him from balconies and rooftops. He arrived at Colómbia around 9:00 P.M. and proceeded to the grandstand facing the parade ground. From the same platform once occupied by Fulgencio Batista, Castro addressed a crowd of 30,000, with radio and television stations broadcasting live.

Although Castro called for the unity of all revolutionary forces, he credited his rebel army for the victory. At that moment, rebel forces of the DRE were in Havana, and they were in no hurry to surrender their arms. Fidel wanted to consolidate the rebel victory, which meant that all anti-Batista forces would have to recognize his leadership, a delicate point that Castro made rather forcefully, energized by the crowd. At one point he turned to Camilo Cienfuegos, the most beloved barbudo, and asked: "Am I doing all right, Camilo?" Camilo replied: "You are doing all right Fidel." The crowd roared its approval and Fidel delivered even more. Toward the end of the speech, somebody released two white doves, one of which came to rest on Castro's shoulder. Thousands in the audience fell on their knees, acknowledging the presence of the revered symbol of the savior in Afro-Cuban religious beliefs. To them, the dove affirmed Castro as the one chosen to redeem Cuba, the person who would deliver them from all the sins of the past. Even the conservative *Diario de la Marina* hailed the moment as an "act of providence."

If any divinity intervened, it only confirmed the power Castro had already acquired. When Castro entered Havana, his rebel commanders had already taken control of Cuba's key military installations, the police force, and secret service, thereby depriving the defenders of the old order with any hope of resisting revolutionary change. The liberals and moderates who had allied with Fidel in opposition to Batista could not match the organizational strength or popularity of Fidel—no doves had landed on their shoulders. Not even José Martí had received such a blessing. In Castro and the young revolutionaries, Cubans vested their hopes for substantial political, economic, and social reform. Martí, Grau, Chibás and others before him had promised revolution and failed to deliver it, but this time, Castro emphasized, the revolution was for real.

CONSOLIDATING THE REVOLUTION, 1959–1960

The first government of the revolution represented all the groups that had contributed to the overthrow of Batista. President Manuel Urrutia appointed a cabinet that included highly respected moderates and liberals unaffiliated with the 26th of July Movement, including José Miró Cardona as prime minister and Roberto Agramonte as foreign minister. The fidelistas were represented in the cabinet by Faustino Perez and Armando Hart, creating the impression that Castro would collaborate with other political organizations in a democratic government. At the same time, the people supported a thorough demolition of the old order. The new government dissolved Batista's congress, abolished all political parties, and postponed elections for eighteen months. Even ex-president Prío, the man deposed by Batista in 1952, accepted the abolition of the old political system and a new government that would govern by decree indefinitely. *Revolución*, the official newspaper of the 26th of July Movement, proudly announced: "We finish with all the vices of the past, all the old political games."

Despite the popular cynicism generated by decades of gangsterism, political corruption, mass poverty, and economic stagnation, the Cuban people had not lost faith in Cuba Libre. Castro called on them to redeem the nation using passionate rhetoric borrowed from Martí, generating a popular optimism that had been absent from Cuban politics for more than two decades. He spoke of political freedom, national sovereignty, economic opportunity, and social justice like many before him, but having led his rebel army to victory over a superior enemy, his promises had credibility. Castro had already accomplished what most people had considered impossible, and the majority of Cubans supported him enthusiastically. Within weeks it became evident that the seat of political power was not Urrutia's office in the presidential palace, but Fidel Castro's suite on the 23rd floor of the Havana Hilton, where the *Máximo Líder*—as he was already being called—issued the directives that guided the revolutionary process. Fidel ended all pretenses in mid-February by having himself named Prime Minister to replace Miró Cardona.

There were, in effect, two governments operating during the first months of the revolution. The official government, led by President Urrutia, administered the state bureaucracy; the unofficial government, led by Comandante Castro, plotted revolution. With Urrutia providing a moderate cover for the regime, Castro purged the old army and created a new one under the command of his loyalists. The purge took place quickly, led by Raúl Castro and Che Guevara, who presided over the trials and executions of hundreds of persons over the next six months. The circus-like atmosphere of some trials, particularly the one televised live from the sports palace, drew international criticism. Castro condemned the hypocrisy of the critics who had raised no voices in opposition to Batista's torture chambers. Hundreds of thousands roared their approval of the executions, a grisly first step in the consolidation of the revolution.

Castro quickly assaulted every remnant of the old order. He slashed monthly rents, reduced telephone rates, increased wages for virtually all workers, eliminated racial segregation, and seized property owned by all former Batista officials. Workers, peasants, and the unemployed received immediate and direct government assistance, while the upper and middle classes grew increasingly alarmed at Fidel's apparent determination to enact a revolution much more radical than they had anticipated.

As Castro publicly proclaimed his intentions to restore democracy, he pursued a revolutionary strategy designed by his top comandantes and his new allies among the Soviet-style communists in the *Partido Socialista Popular* (PSP, Popular Socialist Party). The PSP had endorsed the insurrection as late as the fall of 1958, but the party emerged in a strong position after January 1, 1959. Che Guevara and Raúl Castro sympathized with the Marxist-Leninist doctrines of the party, and Castro could hardly ignore the practical value of a political alliance with a well-disciplined organization with several thousand members. Castro insisted, however, that the old communists had to accept his leadership of a new party that promoted his brand of revolution, not Soviet doctrine.

Castro and Che knew that they had to prepare the road for revolution or risk having it killed in its infancy. From the collapse of the Guatemalan revolution in 1954 they derived three principle lessons that they subsequently applied to the consolidation of the Cuban revolution. To carry out a radical revolution, Castro decided to: 1) purge the old army and replace it with one loyal to the revolution; 2) enact a comprehensive land reform; and 3) organize civilian militias. Having come into power by armed struggle, the Cuban revolutionaries were determined to defend their revolutionary programs against U.S. intervention.

Thus, while Fidel Castro publicly embraced democracy and moderation, he privately prepared for a confrontation with his Cuban opponents and their North American allies. A hint of his radical intentions came in early April, when he announced new conditions for the scheduling of elections.

"We want that when elections come . . . that everybody be working here, that the agrarian reform be a reality . . . that all the children have a school . . . that all families have access to hospitals . . . that every Cuban know his rights and his duties, that every Cuban know how to read and write. . . . Then, we can have truly democratic elections!"

Still, when Castro traveled unofficially to the United States in April 1959, the American media and the general public treated him like a conquering hero. He paid his respects at the Lincoln memorial and publicly promised to respect a free press and hold elections. When asked directly, he denied that he was a communist. He could not tell all this to President Eisenhower because he was out of town, a snub that Fidel would remember. Vice President Richard Nixon, who had earned a reputation as a rabid anti-communist, met privately with Fidel to assess the impulsive young leader. Castro did not even ask for economic assistance. He was not going to request anything from Washington other than respect, and that was an unprecedented assertion of Cuban nationalism. Nixon, however, quickly concluded that Castro was a dangerous communist who would have to be removed.

When Castro returned to Cuba in early May, the pace of revolutionary change accelerated under the slogan of "revolution first, elections later." On May 17, 1959, Castro signed the agrarian reform bill into law at his old headquarters in the Sierra Maestra. Che Guevara, Antonio Nuñez Jiménez, and PSP leaders, the most radical members of the revolutionary coalition, had drafted the law. Humberto Sorí Marín, the minister of agriculture, had not even seen the bill before Castro approved it. The law authorized the nationalization of sugar and rice plantations, and cattle estates larger than 3,300 acres, with compensation in twenty-year bonds bearing 4.5 percent interest. Foreign companies could own estates only if the government determined that their operations served the national interest. The expropriated lands would be reorganized as cooperatives under the management of a newly created Institute of Agrarian Reform (INRA) and distributed in plots of 67 acres to selected families.

Castro became president of INRA and Antonio Nuñez Jiménez its executive director, their offices located in a fourteen-story building on the recently completed Plaza Cívica, built by Batista as a new seat of government. Castro appropriately renamed the vast square the *Plaza de la Revolución*, and it quickly became the heart of the real revolution. There, Castro convened mass meetings of hundreds of thousands of peasants and rural workers, beneficiaries of the agrarian reform. INRA and the army operated as a single entity in service of the revolution, confiscating estates, managing the properties, and driving off former landlords. By the end of 1959, INRA had become the largest land and cattle owner in the nation. Former sugar plantations, cattle ranches, and tobacco farms were converted into state cooperatives. Cane cutters and peasants, the underprivileged in old Cuba, were now the privileged masses in revolutionary Cuba.

The moderates and liberals who opposed the radicalization of the revolution found themselves out of office or in exile, beginning with President Urrutia. Castro deposed him and replaced him with Osvaldo Dorticós in July. In October, Comandante Huber Matos, military commander of Camagüey Province and a hero of the revolution, was arrested and convicted for counterrevolutionary activities because he too had protested the growing communist influence. The radical elements of the 26th of July Movement and the PSP obviously held the upper hand because they controlled the army and enjoyed the support of the masses. The moderates had no institutionalized base of support, little unity, and no recognized leader. All they could do was protest, and twelve of the twenty-one cabinet ministers appointed in January had resigned by the end of the year. The wildly popular Camilo Cienfuegos, who was rumored to be anti-communist as well, died in a mysterious plane crash in October, eliminating the dim prospect that he would arrest the radicalization of the revolution.

With the arrival in Cuba of Soviet premier Anastas Mikoyan in February 1960, Castro went public with his plans to radicalize the revolution. By establishing relations with the Union of Soviet Socialist Republics (USSR), the archenemy of the United States in the Cold War, Castro sent a clear message that he intended to break Cuba out of the American orbit. At the end of a nine-day visit, Mikoyan signed a treaty by which the USSR would purchase 1 million tons of Cuban sugar per year for the next four years, on top of $100 million in credits offered to Cuba for the acquisition of materials and technical assistance. Two months later the Soviets agreed to sell crude oil to Cuba at below market prices. The prospect of a Soviet ally ninety miles away from the American mainland naturally alarmed the United States. On March 17, 1960, President Eisenhower authorized the CIA to implement a covert program to overthrow Castro and terminate the revolution.

DEFINING THE REVOLUTION, 1960–1961

The radical course of the Cuban revolution emerged from and was shaped by pressures from the sectors of Cuban society with the least to lose and the most to gain. Half a million urban workers pushed their union demands on employers and the government; 600,000 agricultural workers demanded better working conditions and higher pay; 665,000 unemployed and underemployed men and women demanded immediate and substantial social and economic reforms; 220,000 peasants demanded land of their own and the means to defend it. They were determined to carry out the "real revolution" that Castro had promised.

Now Castro had to deliver on the promises that he had made to the masses or risk being overthrown by the counter-revolutionary movement that his radical reforms naturally generated. He gained political strength and secured the revolution by organizing and mobilizing the masses, making it possible if not necessary to steer the revolution sharply to the left, away from the middle- to upper-class people who had also participated in and supported the insurrection. Unlike so many of his predecessors, including Grau and Chibás, Castro recognized the power and the potential of the masses, a latent political force that no previous revolutionary leader had ever incorporated into the governing coalition. He boldly gained control of or won the support of the masses by *delivering* on promises such as land reform, health care, education, and higher wages to the most underprivileged sectors of Cuban society—not simply through inspiring rhetoric.

As the masses pulled Castro further and further to the left, the United States pushed him in that same direction. Every new revolutionary proclamation produced a hostile response in the United States, which in turn generated more anti-American hostility among the people. Every time the United States criticized Castro, the masses turned out to praise and defend him. Showing no fear of American military power, Fidel orchestrated a political slugfest that forced two American administrations to adopt hostile policies that offended Cuban nationalists and only accelerated the radicalization of the revolution. The United States did not push Castro anywhere he probably did not want to go anyway, but the policies of two American presidents certainly did nothing to retard the radicalization of the revolution.

Cuban-U.S. relations deteriorated rapidly in the summer of 1960, in a degenerative cycle of action and reaction that led to war. In June, the Cuban government asked foreign oil refineries to process the crude oil imported from the Soviet Union. Shell, Esso, and Texaco refused. The government then nationalized all three refineries. In response, the U.S. Congress authorized the president to eliminate Cuba's remaining sugar quota. Cuba retaliated on July 5 by nationalizing all American businesses and commercial property. President Eisenhower responded the next day by canceling the 700,000 tons of sugar remaining in Cuba's quota for 1960. Cuba's new Soviet friends immediately announced that they would purchase the 700,000 tons eliminated by the Americans. To make it worse for the Americans, on July 23 communist China agreed to purchase 500,000 tons of Cuban sugar each year for five years. In one hot summer month, Cuba bolted out of the American sphere of influence and joined the Communist bloc.

Castro's prestige among nationalists and revolutionaries only increased as he confronted a hostile United States. On September 17, 1960, he defied the United States again, nationalizing all American banks on the island, including Chase Manhattan and the First National City Bank of New York. The next day Castro arrived in New York to address the United Nations General Assembly. During his stay, he met with Soviet Premier Nikita Khrushchev, who gave the Cuban leader a big bear hug, a most public demonstration of the new balance of power in the Caribbean. The United States could not ignore the fact that a former dependency had aligned itself with its enemy, giving the Soviets a revolutionary partner in a region traditionally dominated by the Americans.

The pace of revolutionary change in Cuba far exceeded the expectations of the Soviets. Castro aimed for nothing less than the socialization of Cuba within two years, a feat never accomplished by any revolutionary regime anywhere in the world. The enactment of an Urban Reform Law on October 13, 1960, authorized the nationalization of 382 locally owned firms, including sugar mills, banks, and factories. The inevitable United States retaliation came on October 19, when Eisenhower imposed a partial economic embargo on Cuba that excluded food and medicine. Castro then nationalized all remaining American properties on the island, raising the total value of confiscated American properties to $1 billion. With American investors clamoring for just compensation or U.S. intervention, the diplomatic maneuvering came to an end on January 3, 1961, when the United States severed diplomatic relations with Cuba.

By this time, hundreds of thousands of Cubans had taken refuge in the United States, most of them settling in the Miami area. A minority of them represented the batistianos; most of them represented the white, politically moderate factions of the urban middle and upper classes. Castro's revolutionary program had deprived them of their homes and businesses, and in many cases had divided their families. They preferred exile in southern Florida to life in a communist society for which they had never fought. They left their beloved island feeling betrayed by yet another politician who had once spoken so eloquently of national redemption. Many of them had supported the revolution; some had even fought in or raised money for Castro's rebel army. They arrived in Miami thinking that they were temporary residents in a foreign land, for they were determined to overthrow Castro and return to their homeland and reclaim their livelihoods and property.

By early 1961, Castro already faced a formidable counter-revolutionary rebellion in the Escambray Mountains of southern Las Villas Province. As many as 5,000 anti-communists took up arms and tried to use guerrilla strategies and tactics against the revolution. Castro and Guevara, now experts in guerrilla warfare, knew the terrain and how to exploit the weaknesses of a guerrilla army in its formative phase. They deployed the recently organized militias to establish a cordon around the guerrilla bases in the mountains. Then, Castro and Che, occasionally taking command in the field, hunted down and destroyed the counter-revolutionary bands. By March 1961, the government forces had virtually eliminated the rebels in the Escambray area.

The destruction of these guerrilla bands posed a serious threat to the CIA's plan to overthrow Castro. The plan approved by President Kennedy called for 1,500 exiles to invade the island, establish a beachhead, and coordinate an armed struggle against Castro with all opposition elements, particularly the guerrillas operating in the Escambray. The United States would then recognize a provisional government and offer military assistance to it. Without the counter-revolutionary bands in the Escambray, the invasion forces would have to face Castro's revolutionary forces on their own.

Castro and Che had prepared Cuba precisely for this moment. They had purged the old army and created a new one, with as many as 50,000 men ready to defend the revolution. In addition, they had organized 200,000 men and women into civilian militias commanded by loyal fidelistas. They had also established Committees for the Defense of the Revolution to monitor revolutionary vigilance in neighborhoods and workplaces. They had brought in Soviet arms, ammunition, and anti-aircraft guns to augment their firepower. They had infiltrated Cuban intelligence agents into the Miami exile community. The 1,500 men in the invasion force faced a powerful, united, and determined enemy, one not likely to run for cover when the guns started firing. On March 28, Che Guevara warned that the invaders would find millions of men, women, and children fighting against them from every house and trench on the island. The next day, Fidel and Che played a round of golf at the Havana Country Club, an odd demonstration of supreme confidence.

President Kennedy was not as confident. He had accepted the covert plan from the previous administration primarily because of its feared and respected architects, CIA Director Allen Dulles and Director of Operations Richard Bissell, both of whom assured him that it would succeed. They based their covert plans on the assumption that Castro was unpopular, for they expected the invasion to trigger a spontaneous popular uprising against the revolutionary government. They also counted on air strikes to destroy or at least ground Cuba's tiny air force. Cuban pilots flying American planes would have to take out Castro's twenty-four antiquated American planes before the invasion; if the invasion force did not have control of the skies, Castro's pilots could wreak havoc on them. But Kennedy had rejected an airborne attack and amphibious landing near Trinidad, on the southern coast of Las Villas Province, because it was "too loud." He did not want American forces engaged in combat, determined to maintain the illusion that the invasion was a Cuban operation. He approved a "quiet" invasion at the *Bahía de Cochinos* (Bay of Pigs) on condition that no U.S. military forces would be involved.

The change from Trinidad to the Bay of Pigs left the CIA planners without a viable contingency plan. Only one main road led to and from the Playa Girón, an isolated beach on the southern coast of Havana Province, surrounded by a swamp, and the Escambray Mountains were too far away to offer any refuge to the invaders. If the pre-invasion air strikes by the exiles' air force failed to knock out the Cuban air force, the 1,500 men would be stranded on the beach. And if they expected Kennedy to authorize a U.S. airstrike, they would soon be disappointed. If they managed to break through Cuban defenses, they still needed help from a popular uprising to defeat Castro's revolutionary army and militia. But given that the counter-revolutionary bands had already been defeated in Las Villas Province, no domestic rebellion was likely to occur.

Nevertheless, the counter-revolutionaries went forward, knowing that they faced long odds and a powerful foe. At dawn on April 15, six B-26 bombers piloted by Cubans attacked two air bases outside of Havana and another in Santiago. The bombers failed to take out Castro's air force, leaving Castro with eight planes and seven pilots. The magnitude of the attacks suggested that an invasion was imminent, though the Cubans still did not know exactly where the invasion force would land. Castro mobilized all his forces to defeat the exile force wherever it landed, determined to prevent the United States from establishing a provisional government on Cuban soil.

In the early morning hours of Monday, April 17, approximately 1,500 men landed at Playa Girón. A militia battalion met the invaders and Castro quickly dispatched his forces to annihilate them. Castro's air force attacked first, sinking two freighters and forcing the support vessels to withdraw. With the exiles stranded on the beach, Castro brought in his tanks and heavy artillery to finish them off. As the Cuban army pounded the invasion force, its commander, Lieutenant Pepé San Román, called on the CIA to authorize more airstrikes. Even though Kennedy had made it clear to the CIA that he would not authorize the use of American forces, neither the exiles nor the CIA planners could imagine that he would allow Castro to defeat the invading army. Kennedy, however, would not authorize a second air strike by Cuban or American pilots, determined to maintain the fiction that it was a Cuban operation, not an American act of war.

Less than forty-eight hours after landing on Cuban soil, the exiles were pinned down. Facing an onslaught from Cuban tanks, artillery, and airplanes, the invaders surrendered at dusk on April 19. The revolutionary army and militias captured 1,186 men and killed 107 while losing only 161. The invasion attempt gave Castro the pretext to eliminate all opposition to his regime. By the end of April the government had imprisoned an estimated 100,000 people. Most were released and allowed to leave the island, and the exodus of Cuban refugees to south Florida escalated. Castro had killed, imprisoned, or exiled his opponents. Feeling secure in his position, he announced on May 1, 1961: "this is a socialist revolution." Later that year, things took another sharp turn, as Castro proclaimed: "I am a Marxist-Leninist, and I shall be one until the last day of my life."

DEFENDING THE REVOLUTION, 1961–1962

Castro's public confession of his socialist identity had little impact on the political affiliation of the hundreds of thousands of Cubans who served in the militias, CDR's, unions, and other revolutionary organizations. Of course, a few intellectuals had studied Marxist-Leninist doctrines, but Castro had already won their support by carrying out a sweeping land reform, nationalizing American-owned properties, and closing the casinos. Perhaps more important, he was the first Cuban leader to defeat an American intervention. The political allegiance of the workers and peasants was not bought cheaply, but they cared less about ideological abstractions and more about practical reforms, having heard enough political rhetoric in their lives. They knew enough about José Martí and even a little of Karl Marx, but neither man had actually redistributed wealth and power. If Castro was socialist, many of them concluded, then they were socialist too.

The revolutionary leaders estimated that there were nearly 1 million illiterates on the island, representing 50 percent of the rural population. Mindful of Martí's dictum: "to be literate is to be free," Castro declared 1961 the year of education. In the spring, amidst all the careful preparations to defend the revolution, the government launched a campaign to eradicate illiteracy within a year, an ambitious goal that reflected the unbridled optimism of the revolutionaries. To carry out the project, the government organized more than 270,000 students, workers, and professionals into four large literacy brigades and dispatched them throughout the island to teach all Cubans to read and write. The *brigadistas* lived and worked with rural families during the day and taught them how to read at night. By 1962, the government reported that the adult literacy rate had increased to 96 percent, the highest in Latin America.

The literacy campaign constituted part of a larger effort to reform the entire educational system and give all Cubans equal access to schools. Under the direction of Minister of Education Armando Hart, who established his headquarters at Batista's old Camp Colombia, the government launched a second educational program in 1962. The "Third Grade Campaign" offered educational opportunities to adult Cubans who had had no previous formal education, as did the next project, the "Battle for the Sixth Grade." Although the purpose and content of the educational programs clearly served the revolution, the campaigns provided 800,000 adult Cubans with a basic education. Castro had converted education from a privilege to a right.

While peasants, poor workers, and illiterate adults received tangible benefits from the revolutionary government, middle- to upper-class professionals were leaving the island. The revolutionary government had to replace nearly the entire professional class, a task made even more difficult by the loss of teachers and university professors to train them. To compensate for the loss of doctors, lawyers, and engineers, the educational system had to steer students into careers that had previously been dominated by white, upper-class males. Women and minorities pursued professional degrees like never before. The revolution in education thereby reinforced the social transformation generated by other reforms.

The United States government, particularly the policymakers in the CIA, ignored or dismissed the political significance of the sweeping social and economic reforms implemented by the revolutionary government. By redistributing lands and expanding educational opportunities, the Cuban government solidified its base of support, and that result was not unanticipated by Castro. The number of Cubans willing to defend the revolution probably increased faster than the numbers of Cubans willing to fight against it. The counterrevolutionary forces had not been crushed completely by the dismal failure at the Bay of Pigs, but their power was much reduced by the fact that so many of them were either in prison or exile.

No counter-revolutionary movement could possibly succeed without a direct military intervention by the United States, which Castro fully expected

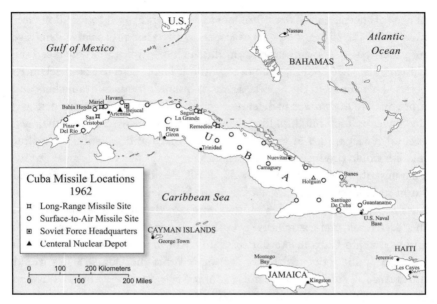

Cuba Missile Locations
1962

¤ Long-Range Missile Site
o Surface-to-Air Missile Site
▣ Soviet Force Headquarters
▲ Centeral Nuclear Depot

after the Bay of Pigs. In November 1961, President Kennedy authorized another covert program against Cuba, this one dubbed Operation Mongoose. The object of Mongoose was to get rid of Castro, with assassination an implicit option alongside economic sabotage, guerrilla operations, and political propaganda. Beginning in early 1962, the CIA infiltrated teams of agents into Cuba. Within months, counter-revolutionary guerrilla bands were operating in Las Villas and Pinar del Río Provinces. Saboteurs targeted hundreds of economic facilities throughout the island while assassins went after Castro, Che Geuvara, and Raúl Castro. In desperation, the CIA hired mafia gunmen and tried a number of bizarre schemes to get rid of Castro, including the old exploding cigar trick.

The United States justified its covert actions against Castro partly on the grounds that he represented a threat to the security of the Americas. Cuba's turn toward socialism and an alliance with the Soviet Union resulted in its expulsion from the Organization of American States in January 1962. In retaliation, Castro threatened to sow the seeds of revolution throughout the Americas. In the declaration of Havana on February 4, 1962, he announced that "the duty of every revolutionary is to make the revolution. . . . The revolution will triumph in America and throughout the world." Castro again made good on his pledge, offering training, inspiration, and material support for guerrilla groups operating in virtually every Latin American nation.

As the conflict between Cuba and the United States grew more tense and ominous, the Soviets became concerned about their ability to defend their new ally. Thereafter, in May 1962, Soviet leaders proposed to install nuclear missiles on the island. The Cuban leaders favored less provocative defensive measures, but the Soviets insisted on the nuclear missiles and convinced the Cubans that they could be deployed without being detected by the United States. That summer, the Soviets began to install forty missile launchers and more than 40,000 troops to defend them. The United States quickly detected the Soviet military buildup. In early September, Kennedy criticized the presence of Soviet troops in Cuba and warned that the installation of nuclear missiles would produce the "gravest issues."

Just after 7 P.M. on October 22, 1962, President Kennedy announced "unmistakable evidence has established the fact that a series of offensive missile sites is now in preparation on that imprisoned island." To bring a halt to this "secret, swift, and extraordinary buildup," Kennedy imposed a naval "quarantine" around Cuba to prevent the delivery of more offensive weapons. To leave no doubt about his resolve, he warned that the United States would unleash "a full retaliatory response upon the Soviet Union" if any missile were fired from Cuba against any American republic.

The worst fears of the Cuban revolutionaries had come true. The United States had discovered the Soviet plot, leaving them dangling between the two nuclear superpowers. Fortunately, cooler heads prevailed on October 24, when Soviet ships laden with more missiles did not challenge American warships on the quarantine line. The so-called Cuban Missile Crisis, however, had not yet passed, for Kennedy demanded the immediate cessation of all work on the missile sites and the return of the missiles to the Soviet Union. Castro, absolutely convinced that Cuba had a legal right to install the weapons, would not even accept United Nations inspection of Cuban territory, warning that "Anyone who wants to inspect Cuba had better come prepared to fight their way in."

If the Soviets did not remove the missiles the Kennedy administration was prepared to destroy them. An air strike was not likely to hit all the targets, even though the Pentagon programmed a total of 1,190 air sorties on the first day of a prospective attack on Cuba. To destroy completely the missile sites, the Pentagon planned to send in 140,000 troops. The Cuban army put 270,000 troops on full alert and mobilized 300,000 militia members, and Castro expected that Soviet troops and fighters would defend their Cuban allies. As evening fell on October 27, all evidence indicated that an American invasion was imminent.

On Sunday morning, October 28, Fidel Castro received a phone call from Carlos Franqui, editor of *Revolución*, who asked for his response to the latest news. "What news?" Fidel asked. Fidel had not yet heard that Khrushchev had ordered the withdrawal of all Soviet missiles in exchange for Kennedy's pledge not to invade Cuba. Fidel exploded in anger, feeling betrayed by Khrushchev, who had reached a secret agreement with Kennedy without consulting him. He would have wanted more concessions from the United States, like an end to the economic blockade and the termination of all subversive activities directed against Cuba. Castro had expected to be treated like a friend and ally, but the Soviets had ignored him.

For their part, the Soviets and Americans had stepped back from the brink of what might have been an all-out nuclear war. The Americans had not known that the Soviet commanders had tactical nuclear missiles on the island. If the Americans had landed, the Soviet commanders might have given the order to fire them to prevent being overwhelmed by the U.S. forces. If that had occurred, Kennedy probably would have retaliated with a full nuclear strike against the Soviet Union, triggering in turn, a Soviet strike on the United States. Nothing would have been left of Cuba. Castro and Cuba, even the world, stood on the edge of disaster and still Fidel could only think of how both superpowers had failed to treat Cuba with the respect due a sovereign nation.

During the missile crisis the Soviets learned what American authorities had failed to appreciate during the previous six decades: the nationalistic impulses in the Cuban character were extraordinary, and in the process of defining and defending the Cuban revolution in the face of determined American opposition, this sense of nationalism or Cubanidad grew even more intense. The revolutionaries had defeated Batista and consolidated a socialist revolution in a region once considered off-limits even by their Soviet allies. They had easily defeated the CIA and the Cuban exiles at the Bay of Pigs; they had gone to the brink of nuclear war with the Americans. Castro, with only his pride hurt during a series of international crises, could now legitimately claim victory over one dictator and two American presidents. A spirit of optimism prevailed among the Cubans that remained on the island. Fidel still had not been defeated by anybody. The peasants, workers, and Afro-Cubans who supported him and benefited from the revolution did not expect him to lose.

REVOLUTION WITH PACHANGA, 1963–1970

In the fall of 1959, Fidel Castro convened a meeting of his top advisers to discuss the resignation of Felipe Pazos, the respected economist who had served as president of the National Bank. Fidel needed another economist to replace Pazos. "Is anybody an economist?" he asked. To Fidel's surprise, Che raised his hand. So Castro appointed him president of the National Bank. After the meeting, Fidel put his arm around Che as they walked out of the office. "Che,

I didn't know you were an economist!" Che was stunned: "Economist! I thought you said Communist!"

Fidel and Che repeated this joke so often that it has gone down in revolutionary lore as fact. Even if the story is apocryphal, it reflected the improvisational and unorthodox approach that characterized the Cuban revolution in the 1960s. Che Guevara, trained as a medical doctor in Argentina, served the Cuban revolution as the president of the National Bank and the Minister of Industry from 1959 until his departure in 1965. A man with no formal training in economics occupied two posts from which he designed Cuba's development strategy. To Che and the revolutionaries, the president's office in the National Bank was just another trench in the struggle for Cuba's liberation.

The revolutionaries exuded confidence, the masses responded with equal enthusiasm, and the fervor of both intensified. The objective conditions for revolution, such as the size of the industrial workforce, did not matter as much as the spirit and dedication of the workers. With determination and hard work, the Cuban revolutionaries believed that they could accomplish just about anything. They had overthrown a dictatorship and defeated the counter-revolutionary movements supported by the United States. Firmly established in power by 1963, the Cuban revolutionaries felt that they had earned the right to pursue their own policies, even if they contradicted Soviet doctrines. They would make their revolution with *pachanga*, a short-lived popular dance craze of the early 1960s. Idealistic and optimistic, the leaders of the Cuban revolution believed that they would develop a unique brand of socialism in Cuba, one reflecting the island's history, geography, society, and culture. Communism in Cuba would dance to a different rhythm, the beat of the tropics.

With Che Guevara in command of the economy, first as president of the National Bank then as Minister of Industry, economic development pursued an unorthodox and ambitious track. He intended to create a utopian society in which the exploitation of man by man ceased to exist. Following the dictum of Marx, "from each according to his ability, to each according to his need," the revolutionaries intended to establish an egalitarian system of socialist production that would distribute goods and services equitably. To that end, the revolutionary government confiscated virtually all private properties and socialized the means of production. The state managed and directed the nation's development to stimulate production, promote economic diversification, reduce Cuba's dependence on foreign trade and investment, promote full employment, and redistribute income.

The Cubans engaged in a rigorous debate about their economic objectives and the means of promoting the goals of diversification, independence, and redistribution. Orthodox communists, led by Carlos Rafael Rodríguez, argued that the construction of socialism took careful planning and patience, based on the Soviet experience. Cuba, lacking the objective conditions for a rapid transition to socialism, would have to develop its industrial base and engineer a transition through three distinct phases leading ultimately to the construction of communism. Rodríguez and the other orthodox communists argued that elements of capitalist policy and institutions would have to remain in place during the construction of socialism.

In opposition, a group of idealists led by Che Guevara argued that Cuba possessed the subjective conditions to skip through the transitional socialist stage between capitalism and communism and could therefore build socialism and communism simultaneously. The high level of revolutionary consciousness already alive in the workers and peasants would allow Cuba to accomplish the impossible. Che advocated highly centralized planning, the complete elimination of private enterprise, and the elimination of all market incentives, including the profit motive. Determined to destroy all vestiges of the free market, he refused to use capitalist incentives to build communism. The success of Guevara's model required the creation of a "New Man," unselfish and patriotic, frugal and hard working, who would sacrifice his personal interests for the promotion of the general welfare. This New Man would be moved to higher rates of productivity and greater efficiency solely through the use of moral incentives. Wage differentials in all sectors would be completely eliminated; everybody would earn the same wage, regardless of profession, training, or expertise. Eventually there would not even be a need for money; goods and services would be produced and exchanged according to ability and need.

By the end of 1965 the "Great Debate" between Guevara and Rodríguez had ended, with Castro leaning toward the adoption of Guevara's radical position. In the spring of 1968 the government launched another revolutionary offensive in which the state took control of 56,000 small businesses, including bars, restaurants, repair shops, and even street vendors. At the same time, the state increased its share of the agricultural sector to 70 percent and renewed its emphasis on sugar production and exports. The state assumed complete command of the economy and virtually eliminated all vestiges of private enterprise.

In 1965 the Soviets signed a five-year agreement to increase purchases of Cuban sugar by 150 percent, at a higher price than they had paid in the previous accord. The Cuban government intended to divert the revenues generated by higher sugar exports to diversify the economy. As a result, Castro arbitrarily set the grandiose target of harvesting 10 million tons of sugar in 1970, nearly

3 million tons higher than the previous record. The government mobilized the entire workforce to bring in the record harvest, sending "volunteer" students and workers into the cane fields with machetes. As it happened, the Cubans harvested only 8.5 million tons—a record crop that fell only 15 percent below the target—a shortcoming that Castro painfully confessed to a crowd in the Plaza de la Revolución.

The radical experiment ended in a disappointing failure. The gains in the sugar industry came at the expense of other economic sectors. Productivity generally declined and consumer goods grew scare as per capita growth rates declined. The surge in industrial productivity never occurred; after reaching peak levels in 1967, productivity actually declined. The efforts to create a "New Man" as Cuba built socialism and communism simultaneously failed. According to economist Carmelo Mesa-Lago, "the failure of both the development strategy and model of economic organization tried in 1966–70 . . . forced the Cuban leadership to a significant shift in the 1970s."

The government also attempted to initiate a revolution with pachanga in social and cultural affairs. Guevara, the most articulate exponent of utopian dreams, argued that the revolution would liberate the individual. The creation of a socialist society in Cuba would unleash the potential of all people, allowing arts and letters to flourish in revolutionary Cuba. Guevara argued that with the development of a socialist society, "man begins to liberate his thought from the bothersome fact that presupposes the need to satisfy his animal needs through work. He begins to see himself portrayed in his work and to understand its human magnitude through the created object, through the work carried out."

Some Cuban intellectuals, such as the renowned Afro-Cuban poet Nicolás Guillén, and the famed novelist Alejo Carpentier, supported the revolutionary ambitions and policies of the government. Guillén became the president of the Union of Writers and Artists (UNEAC) and Carpentier served as a diplomatic representative in France. Both men supported the general proposition that Cuban artists, writers, and intellectuals had the right to produce what they wanted, but they did not have the right to criticize the revolution. In a 1961 address, Castro explained the limits on intellectual activity in the dictum: "within the revolution, everything; against the revolution, nothing."

Many famous Cuban artists refused to accept the new limits on artistic activity. Celia Cruz, arguably Cuba's most famous singer, expressed her opposition by going into exile, as did the writer Guillermo Cabrera Infante. Some, such as the poet Heberto Padilla, attempted to work within the new guidelines. In 1968 UNEAC awarded Padilla its annual poetry prize, the highest recognition for any Cuban poet. However, Padilla subsequently crossed the limits of tolerable expression and was arrested in 1971 on suspicions of sponsoring counter-revolutionary activities. After a month of badgering and harassment, Padilla was released in exchange for a humiliating and abject public confession of his "reprehensible" sins. The coerced confession of the internationally acclaimed poet demonstrated that freedom of expression did not include the right to express opinions that the state regarded as contrary to the principles of the revolution.

The government asserted control over all the private media, denying its opponents any access to newspapers, radio, television, and film. Government-controlled media dominated by *Granma*, the official newspaper of the Communist party of Cuba, replaced a relatively free and vibrant private press prior to the revolution. Government censors sifted through all news reports, prohibiting the publication of any item that did not serve the interests of the revolution. The result was a print media that provided "facts" without commentary, such as Castro's lengthy speeches without criticism. Castro defended the rigid censorship on the grounds that the revolution could not afford to grant liberties to "that powerful enemy who has tried to destroy the revolution and to drown it in the blood of the people."

At the same time the state restricted freedom of expression, its educational reforms made it possible for a larger segment of the population to express themselves. The revolutionary government provided educational opportunities to Cubans who had never enjoyed such privileges. School enrollments at all levels increased dramatically after 1959, with Cuban schools graduating more women and minorities than ever before. Prior to the revolution, university students, primarily men, pursued degrees in the humanities, social sciences, and the law. After the revolution, the government managed and expanded the university system to channel students into medicine, technology, science, and economics, professions that had suffered a decline in numbers due to post-1959 defections. The humanities, meanwhile, suffered from the lack of relative interest and the restrictions placed on cultural expression by the revolutionary government.

The duty of revolutionaries was, after all, to make revolution, not art. Thus, the government placed a high priority on promoting insurrection throughout Latin America. Communist parties throughout the region had rejected the strategy of armed struggle before 1959 and continued to resist it afterward, despite the example of the Cuban Revolution. While orthodox communists held to the proposition that the conditions for revolution did not yet exist in Latin America, the proponents of revolution with pachanga insisted that they did. According to Che, the Cuban victory over Batista taught Latin American revolutionaries three basic lessons. One, "popular forces can win a war against the army." Two, "it is not necessary to wait until all conditions for making revolution exist; the insurrection can create them." And three, "in underdeveloped America the countryside is the basic area for armed fighting."

Latin American communists, following the Soviet line, argued that only the organized proletariat, with the Communist party as its vanguard, could possibly lead the revolutionary movement. Their analyses revealed that the Latin American proletariat lacked the strength and consciousness required for a revolutionary movement. Given the weaknesses of the proletariat, the Communists devoted their efforts toward organizing labor unions, building political coalitions, and participating in electoral politics while they ignored the rural masses. Castro's successful rebellion, however, had demonstrated the revolutionary potential of the peasants and the virtues of waging guerrilla campaigns from the mountains, beyond the reach of the professional army. Guevara urged revolutionaries not to ignore the struggle of organized workers, but he warned that activists in the cities faced greater dangers than in the countryside. In strategic terms, Che recognized that the countryside offered the ideal terrain for a successful guerrilla campaign; in political terms, Che saw the peasants as revolutionaries, not reactionaries.

In Che Guevara's *Guerrilla Warfare*, Latin Americans found a basic manual in the strategy and tactics of guerrilla warfare. This manual, widely read and discussed, called on revolutionaries everywhere to establish guerrilla fronts in remote mountain bases, with or without the support of the Communist party or the urban proletariat. In time, the guerrilla band would increase in size and expand the scope of its operations by integrating the peasants into the struggle under the banner of agrarian reform. The guerrilla *foco* was only the "embryo" of a regular army and a conventional campaign. Guerrilla warfare, Che argued, was "one of the initial phases of warfare and will develop continuously until the guerrilla army in its steady growth acquires the characteristics of a regular army. At that moment it will be ready to deal final blows to the enemy and to achieve victory. Triumph will always be the product of a regular army, even though its origins are in a guerrilla army."

Initially, Guevara limited the applicability of his doctrines to Caribbean-style dictators like Batista. By 1963 however, he recognized no limits on its applicability and called for armed insurrection in every Latin American nation. He also expanded his perspective to the developing countries of Asia and Africa, continents mired in the same struggle against imperialist exploitation. Fidel Castro and Che Guevara considered it their duty as revolutionaries to support and encourage revolution around the world. By 1965, Che was openly calling on the Soviet Union and China to support liberation movements in Asia, Africa, and Latin America. He explained: "There are no frontiers in this struggle to the death. We cannot remain indifferent in the face of what occurs in any part of the world. A victory for any country against imperialism is our victory, just as any country's defeat is a defeat for all."

In Guevara's "Message to the Tricontinental," he explained the strategy of a global war against imperialism that required the coordination of guerrilla campaigns across three continents. The struggle of the Vietnamese people against the United States was already draining the United States of its resources and morale. If the United States had to fight on two other continents simultaneously, it would inevitably lose ground in the war against communism. Thus, the objective of Che Guevara's tricontinental strategy was to provoke U.S. intervention. He intended to launch guerrilla focos throughout Latin America and Africa. In time, they would grow stronger and compel the United States to intervene militarily. Such intervention would gradually weaken the United States and lead to the ultimate victory of "the people" over imperialism.

Guevara did more than just call on his allies to "create one, two, three Vietnams." Indeed, Che took to the field, first in the Congo and then in Bolivia, to lead a battle to the death against imperialism. He departed Cuba secretly in 1965, fueling rumors that he had had a serious dispute with Fidel Castro. Yet his missions to the Congo and Bolivia had the full support of the Cuban government, as indicated by the money and personnel assigned to these guerrilla fronts. Castro in fact attached great importance to the success of the guerrilla bands organized, trained, or commanded by Che. Che took with him to Bolivia high-ranking members of the Cuban Communist party, and enough supplies and money to mount a serious challenge to an American ally in the heart of South America.

As it happened, Che encountered stiff resistance from the American trained and supplied Bolivian army. He apparently expected the Bolivian army to make the same mistakes committed by Batista's army in Cuba. With American agents providing military advice and critical intelligence, the Bolivians pursued Che Guevara relentlessly, knowing that they could not allow him to establish a guerrilla base in the mountains. Che failed to attract the peasant support he expected and found himself isolated and trapped in a desolate region of southeastern Bolivia. In October 1967, Bolivian Rangers captured and executed him.

The tragic end to Guevara, a handsome and popular symbol of the Cuban revolution, followed by the failure of the sugar harvest in 1970, brought an end to a decade of revolutionary innovation and experimentation. The revolution with pachanga fell far short of its goals in both domestic and foreign affairs. To correct the deficiencies of the revolution, the Cubans changed the course of the revolution and aligned themselves with Soviet economic and foreign policies. The allure of the bearded revolutionaries with their olive-green fatigues had faded, and the future looked much grimmer than the triumphant revolutionaries of 1959 had ever anticipated.

CHAPTER SIX

The Last Revolutionary, 🌿 1970–2005 🌿

*T*housands of Cuban and foreign journalists gathered at José Martí International Airport to welcome Soviet Premier Mikhail Gorbachev on April 2, 1989. No Soviet leader had visited the island since 1974, when Cuban relations with the Soviet Union were at their best. With large economic subsidies and military assistance from the Soviet Union, Fidel Castro had taken the Cuban revolution to its political and economic apogee in the 1970s and 1980s. Castro had no reason to change Cuba's relations with the Soviet Union, but Gorbachev was a reformer. His pursuit of *glasnost'* (openness) in the Soviet Union and Eastern Europe had already initiated political and economic reforms that Castro considered dangerous. Eastern Europe and the Soviet Union itself seemed on the verge of repudiating Marxism and embracing democratic capitalism. Gorbachev's trip to Cuba fueled speculation that he intended to bring this powerful reformist movement to Communist Cuba as well.

Castro, a sixty-three-year-old revolutionary dressed in his customary olive-green fatigues, was now the orthodox communist, a staunch defender of the old order he had once criticized. Cuba had been fully integrated into the Soviet bloc trade network, exporting sugar, nickel, citrus, tobacco, and rum in exchange for oil, machinery, and consumer goods. The trade agreements that regulated this international commerce amounted to economic subsidies worth more than $3 billion per year. Gorbachev, the fifty-eight-year-old Soviet premier dressed in Western-style suits, appeared in Havana as an unorthodox capitalist. He had every reason to modify commercial relations with Cuba because the Soviet Union could no longer afford to subsidize it. Journalist Andres Oppenheimer noted the ironic significance of Gorbachev's arrival in

Havana: "It was a strange scene, as if the roles had reversed: for the first time, Cubans saw an aging Castro greeting a younger, more dynamic Soviet leader."

Over the next three days neither Gorbachev nor Castro gave any public indication of the private discord that now separated the former allies. Gorbachev repeatedly assured the Cubans that he would not impose his political reforms on Castro. Yet in subsequent meetings, Soviet bureaucrats informed Cuban officials that future commercial relations would be conducted on the basis of equality and reciprocity. In practice, this meant that the Cubans would have to begin paying for Soviet goods in dollars. The Soviets would no longer underwrite Cuba's economic development. As Oppenheimer put it: "the party was over."

Within three years of the meeting between Castro and Gorbachev, the Soviet Union had disintegrated and the entire Soviet bloc had disappeared, allowing the United States to claim victory in the Cold War and proclaim that the triumph of capitalism and democracy throughout the world was inevitable and irreversible. The loss of Soviet economic assistance plunged Cuba into the worst economic crisis since the revolution. Yet Castro remained intransigent, refusing to embrace the sweeping political reforms that had swept over Eastern Europe. In 1990 he vowed: "If the USSR were to break up, if the USSR were to disappear, we would continue constructing socialism in our country."

That same year, the Sandinista government of Nicaragua, which had come to power in 1979 with Cuban support, was voted out of office, depriving Cuba of its only ally in the hemisphere. "We are alone—alone—here, in this ocean of capitalism that surrounds us," Castro announced in 1991. The loss of Cuba's Soviet and Nicaraguan allies only seemed to strengthen Castro's determination to hold on to Cuba's socialist experiment. He imposed even greater austerity measures and repressed all domestic and foreign calls for reform. Fifteen years later, Castro was still in power, the last revolutionary in the Western Hemisphere.

THE INSTITUTIONAL REVOLUTION, 1970–1980

The Cuban Revolution never came any closer to fulfilling its socialist ambitions than it did in the 1970s. After a decade of revolutionary experimentation in the 1960s, Castro yielded to Soviet pressure and implemented more conventional domestic and foreign policies under the aegis of a formal Communist party apparatus and an immovable state bureaucracy. In part, the institutionalization of the revolution reflected Castro's recognition that the radical experiment of the 1960s had failed, at home and abroad. The hard reality that the socialist utopia of which the revolutionaries dreamed was only a remote and distant possibility set in, forcing the Cuban leadership to adopt more practical economic policies and institutionalize the revolution along Soviet lines.

Fidel Castro's speech on July 26, 1970, marked the end of the radical experiment and the beginning of the institutionalized revolution. Castro was forced to make an unprecedented admission that he had failed to deliver on one of his promises. Henceforth, Cuba would adopt more pragmatic development policies and work toward realistic economic objectives. At Soviet insistence, the Cubans adopted market reforms to stimulate productivity and increase the supply of consumer goods. In place of Che Guevara's moral incentives, the state offered material incentives such as wage increases and bonuses. State enterprises were given greater autonomy to run their factories and generate profits, which could be returned to productive workers as bonuses. The revolutionary government allowed private enterprise in the tobacco industry, and even allowed small farmers to sell their surpluses at market prices. Self-employment was allowed in occupations such as carpentry, plumbing, and automobile repair. The government maintained an extensive social net that provided free education and health care while guaranteeing a minimum level of sustenance for every person.

The Soviets rewarded Cuba's move toward communist orthodoxy in 1972, when Cuba joined the Council for Mutual Economic Assistance (COMECON), the Soviet Union trading bloc. In joining the Soviet commercial bloc, the Cubans surrendered their goals of diversifying and industrializing the economy. Cuba's role within the Soviet system was to provide tropical goods and services that the Europeans could not produce, primarily sugar, and import the foodstuffs and manufactured products that Cuba could not produce. On the surface the commercial relationships replicated Cuba's economic dependency on the United States during prerevolutionary times. In practice, however, the Soviet Union purchased Cuban sugar at above market prices and sold oil, consumer goods, and other manufactured products at below market prices. The price differential amounted to a significant annual subsidy that allowed the Cuban economy to forego diversification. Thus, the Soviet commercial agreements maintained Cuba's traditional dependence on sugar exports and limited opportunities for the growth of manufacturing.

Soviet economic assistance went even further. Soviet technicians arrived in Cuba to construct or manage public utilities (including a nuclear plant at Cienfuegos), oil refineries, steel mills, sugar refineries, and factories. What little industrialization occurred therefore depended on Soviet bloc equipment and personnel. As long as Cuba remained within the Soviet orbit, however, its friends and allies in the socialist camp would satisfy its manufacturing needs.

As Cuban and Soviet commercial relations expanded, the Cubans created an institutional apparatus that paralleled the Soviet system. The Cubans
were required to draft long-term development strategies and negotiate commercial agreements with their Soviet counterparts. Thus, the Cubans created
a Soviet-like Council of State, Council of Ministers, and dozens of institutes,
committees, and academies that mirrored the Soviet system. Each organization would then deal directly with the appropriate Soviet agency to formulate
and implement development policies.

The culmination of the Cuban reorganization came in 1975 with the
First Congress of the Communist Party of Cuba (PCC). The party had been
formed by the unification of the 26th of July Movement, Directorio
Revolucionario, and the old Popular Socialist Party in the early 1960s. However, the party structure and its relationship with the government was not
formalized until 1975, when the delegates drafted a new constitution that
confirmed Fidel Castro as the maximum leader of the revolution. The constitution established a presidential system of government with power concentrated in a chief executive who presided over a Council of State and Council of
Ministers. It also created, at least on paper, a hierarchical system of representative government known as Popular Power. Cubans would be allowed to elect
representatives to municipal assemblies, which in turn elected delegates to a
regional assembly, which in turn sent representatives to the national assembly.
A limited degree of political participation was allowed at the local level, but
the high officials of the PCC screened candidates, set general policy, and controlled the decision-making apparatus.

The party hierarchy overlapped the government structure and essentially determined the policies that came out of it. The Political Bureau of the
PCC sat at the top of a well-defined party hierarchy, with a secretariat and
central committee below it. Major policy decisions were made in the Political
Bureau, which Castro controlled from its inception. As secretary general of
the PCC, president, and commander in chief, Fidel controlled the party, the
government, and the military. The institutionalization of the revolution did
not diminish the personal power that Fidel Castro held over the party or the
government.

With the party and government institutionalized along Soviet lines, and
Cuba's policies shaped by Soviet bureaucrats and their experiences, the Cuban
revolution offered tangible benefits to people who accepted the limits of the
system and worked within it. The Cuban revolutionaries made substantial
improvements in health care, education, and housing, although whatever ac-
complishments they achieved were due in no small part to Soviet support and
subsidies. Without Soviet assistance, it is likely that the Cuban revolution

would not have achieved the social progress for which the revolutionaries took great pride.

In the area of health care, the government overcame debilitating losses in the early 1960s and made substantial gains in the delivery of medical services to those who could not afford them. Cuba had an excellent corps of medical doctors and facilities before the revolution, but medical services were concentrated in Havana and available only to the middle and upper classes. Vast sectors of the rural population had no access to medical care. The situation worsened after 1959 because so many doctors fled Cuba. It took a decade for the government to train enough new personnel to bring the doctor/population ratio back to the prerevo-lution level (1 per 1,000). At the same time, government spending on hospital construction and clinics, with priority given to areas outside Havana, brought medical services to people with little or no access to health care. Infant mortality rates dropped and life expectancy rose significantly as the Cubans created one of the best health care systems in Latin America.

The revolution's commitment to an egalitarian society was also evident in the government's efforts to eliminate malnutrition. In the early days of the revolution the government instituted a food-rationing system that guaranteed every Cuban a minimum intake of 1,900 calories per day. The family allotment was determined by identifying the specific needs of each household, such as the presence of infants and pregnant women. The ration books provided a basic though monotonous, no-frills diet to each person. Workers could supplement their rations by eating at work-center cafeterias or school lunchrooms.

There was a price to be paid, however, for universal health care, ration books, and education, even though the services were nominally free of charge. The government's political and economic policies drove a large segment of the population, basically the urban middle and upper classes, out of the nation. Doctors, lawyers, professors, businesspeople, shopkeepers and mechanics lost homes, businesses, academic freedom, savings accounts, repair shops, political rights, and economic freedoms. They expressed their opposition to the revolution by fighting or fleeing it in staggering numbers. By 1979 nearly 500,000 Cubans had left the island, most of them settling in south Florida.

Those who remained in Cuba risked imprisonment and death if they opposed the revolutionary regime and its policies. As the revolution moved in a decidedly orthodox direction, repression fell hard on all dissidents. The police could and still can arrest, imprison, and interrogate suspects indefinitely without trial because the government did not and still does not respect the right of habeas corpus. Any attempt by friends or relatives to appeal for the release of a detained person only risks further abuse. Human rights groups and Cuban exile organizations estimated the number of political prisoners in the 1970s between 10,000 and 40,000. The Cuban government rarely divulged any information about its prison system, but the portrait of prison life that has emerged from the accounts of a few survivors tells of systematic abuses and political repression.

To be sure, blacks and the rural poor gained unprecedented educational opportunities, but the Communist party set strict limits on their access to "counter-revolutionary" ideas. While students got their fill of Karl Marx, José Martí, and other acceptable revolutionaries, they did not have unrestricted access to the works of "counter-revolutionary" political philosophers such as Thomas Jefferson. In health care, Cuba has excellent facilities and highly skilled personnel, but the delivery of medical services is hampered by shortages of critical supplies, including medicines that are difficult to obtain because of the U.S. embargo on trade with Cuba.

And Castro was quick to blame most of Cuba's political and economic problems on the economic embargo imposed by the United States, but Cuban mismanagement and Soviet inefficiency also contributed to a lackluster performance in the 1970s. As long as the Soviet Union provided Cuba with oil, foodstuffs, machinery, appliances, medicines and other consumer goods at subsidized prices, the Cuban government could keep the hospitals stocked with medicines, the stores with food, and the schools with books and paper. Soviet economic assistance allowed Cuba to maintain an extensive social safety net that guaranteed an adequate supply of the necessities of life, food, housing, medical care, and education. The low quality of the consumer goods coming from the Soviet bloc did not matter so much to people who had never owned a washing machine, a refrigerator, or a car.

With its economic development underwritten by the Soviet Union, Cuba engaged in an aggressive foreign policy. Following the death of Che Guevara in 1967, the Cuban government scaled back its covert operations around the world. In the late 1970s, as the Cuban economy recovered and political crises erupted in Central America, the government increased its support for revolutionary groups in Nicaragua, El Salvador, and Guatemala. In July 1979, the Sandinistas of Nicaragua, inspired and trained by Cuba in the early 1960s, overthrew the Somoza family dynasty and launched a socialist revolution. The victory represented the first triumph for a revolutionary strategy that Cuba had promoted for twenty years and gave it its only ally in the region. Cuba had provided military assistance to the Sandinistas during their long struggle against the Somozas, and it expanded its support to the Sandinista government throughout the 1980s, providing military and economic assistance as well as doctors and educators.

However, Cuba delivered its greatest military support and scored its most significant victory in Africa. During the Angolan Civil War of 1975–76, Castro sent 36,000 Cuban combat troops to fight alongside the Popular Movement for the Liberation of Angola (PMLA). The Cubans played a decisive role in the victory of the PMLA over troops backed by the United States and South Africa. In 1978, 15,000 Cuban troops fought in Ethiopia to repel a Somalian invasion.

Cuba's commitment to African liberation earned Fidel Castro the respect and support of developing countries in Africa, Asia, and Latin America. Even though Cuba was closely aligned with the Soviet Union, Cuba was selected as the host for the 1979 summit of the Nonaligned Movement, and Fidel Castro was chosen as the chair and spokesman of the organization until 1983. The island country of Cuba had become a major player in global politics, and Cuba was at the height of its power and influence throughout the developing world.

Yet beneath a veneer of stability and prosperity, Cubans still dreamed of political alternatives and challenged Castro's vision of Cuba Libre, which did not include freedom to travel abroad. On April 12, 1980, twelve Cuban nationals stormed through the gates of the Peruvian Embassy in Havana and demanded asylum. The Cuban government, after initially attempting to arrest the dissidents, subsequently announced that anybody wishing to leave the nation could be picked up at the port of Mariel. Friends and relatives in Miami sailed to Cuba in all types of vessels to pick up the refugees. Over the next five months, 125,000 people fled Cuba in what became known as the Mariel boatlift. In contrast to earlier migrations, the refugees came from the poor, working classes, with a large percentage of them blacks and mulattos who had once believed in and benefited from the revolution. Partly as a result, Americans were less sympathetic toward the *Marielitos* than they had been to the post-1959 exiles, who were regarded as successful immigrants.

RACE AND CULTURE IN REVOLUTIONARY CUBA

The Havana Yacht Club in Miramar had been the social refuge of Cuba's aristocracy since its founding in 1886. Without a recommendation from an existing member and the proper background, no amount of money would guarantee any Cuban admission to this exclusive club. As mentioned, the club had even refused to admit President Fulgencio Batista because he did not possess the right social credentials—in other words, he was not white. Racism and racially exclusive institutions definitely existed in prerevolutionary Cuba. Law and custom, however, did not mandate racial segregation in schools, restaurants, and other public institutions. Blacks, whites, and mulattos played on racially integrated baseball teams, lived in the same neighborhoods, and worked side by side in the factories. There was nothing comparable in Cuba to the racial segregation and violence that characterized the southern United States during the era of Jim Crow.

There was, of course, the uprising of the *Partido Independiente de Color* in 1912 and a wave of racially motivated violence that followed. Racial problems existed in Cuba, but public appearances created the impression of relatively harmonious race relations. Blacks and mulattos ran for public office, served in the government, and held high ranks in the army. Yet few organizations or political leaders pressed for reforms designed specifically to promote the cause of racial equality. Various social indicators demonstrated that white Cubans had higher levels of education and income than did Cubans of color. These same people, however, liked to claim that the social disparities did not reflect any discriminatory attitudes toward Cubans of color. If private institutions like the Havana Yacht Club did not have any black members, it was not necessarily a reflection of pervasive racist attitudes.

Racial equality was not a high priority item in the political program of Fidel Castro's 26th of July Movement. The organization did not officially aim to correct any racial inequities, although Cubans of color joined it and fought alongside whites. Some of them, notably Juan Almeida, even rose to the rank of comandante and occupied high positions in the revolutionary government. The objective of the revolutionary leaders was to promote social justice through redistributive measures that would necessarily benefit the poorest people in Cuban society, who just happened to be black and mulatto.

Thus, the abolition of legal discrimination in March 1959, which opened the doors of the Havana Yacht Club and other racially exclusive institutions to persons of color, was not as important to blacks and mulattos as other social and economic reforms that targeted the poor, irrespective of race. The land reform of May 1959, for example, by confiscating estates and distributing lands to the rural poor, provided real and tangible benefits to blacks. The literacy campaign of 1961, while it did not specifically aim at teaching blacks how to read and write, benefited the poor black and mulatto people who had not had the opportunity to attend school. The provision of health care and medical services to the poor similarly extended benefits to Cubans of color.

The revolutionary leaders viewed race relations and the racial problem (to the extent that they even admitted the existence of one) from a Marxist perspective. Castro interpreted racial discrimination as the product of the class conflict that characterized capitalist societies like the United States. By eliminating class conflict, Castro and the others believed, racism and racial conflict would also be eliminated. According to historian Alejandro de la Fuente, "it was assumed [by the leaders] that with the elimination of what they viewed as the causes of racial inequality (private property, class exploitation), racism and racial discrimination would automatically disappear. It would take some time to erase racial prejudice, but the *new man* would not know racism."

Thus, Castro proudly announced in the Second Declaration of Havana in 1962 that the revolution had eliminated racial discrimination. There was no doubt that blacks and mulattos had benefited from the revolution. Before it, the rate of illiteracy among blacks was far greater than the rate among whites. Blacks had less access to higher education than whites, with the result that they were underrepresented in high-paying professions. The literacy campaign of 1961 and the adult education programs that followed it virtually eliminated illiteracy throughout Cuba. Moreover, the revolution opened the university doors to all Cubans regardless of color, allowing blacks to pursue professions previously beyond their reach, such as medicine, law, and engineering. By 1980, blacks and mulattos actually tended to have a slightly higher educational level than whites.

In any event, no decree could eliminate racism in Cuba. After Castro claimed an early victory in the struggle against racial discrimination, race relations became a low priority. Those who dared to raise concerns about racial equality risked being labeled as counter-revolutionaries. Since the revolution allegedly had already triumphed over racism, then anybody who dared to criticize the government for failing to address the needs of blacks and mulattos was deemed counter-revolutionary. "The government had 'solved' the racial problem: to speak about it would only generate problems and create unnecessary divisions, a position close to that of the advocates of racial silence in republican Cuba," de la Fuente explains.

While race was treated as a nonissue in domestic affairs, it became a critical issue in international affairs. Castro frequently condemned racism in the United States and linked his revolutionary movement to the struggle of African Americans for their basic civil rights. Castro's support for African liberation movements, particularly in Angola, contrasted sharply with the foreign policy of the United States, which allied with the apartheid regime of South Africa to oppose the Angolan revolutionaries. Cuban involvement with Africa was portrayed as a reflection of the natural racial and ethnic bonds between the Cubans—defined by Castro as an "Afro-Latin" people—and the Africans. The Cuban revolution was officially committed to the elimination of racism at home and the liberation of Africans and their descendents abroad. As a result of dramatic departures in domestic and foreign policies, Castro earned a strong and loyal following among blacks and mulattos in Cuba.

Nevertheless, one should not be swayed by the appearance of success. The large percentage of blacks and mulattos that left Cuba during the Mariel boatlift certainly reflected growing dissatisfaction with the revolution. Typically, the previous Cuban émigrés were whites from the middle and upper classes; 84 percent of the nearly 1 million Cuban immigrants in the United States in 1980 identified themselves as white. Black Cubans did not find the United States appealing and expected tangible benefits from the revolution. But during the Mariel boatlift of 1980, blacks and mulattos immigrated to the United States in a proportion close to their percentage in the total population (33 percent). Their defection from the revolution suggests that a substantial number of Cubans of color had finally begun to question the benefits of the revolution.

While social indicators such as education, employment, and literacy indicated that Cuba was one of the most racially equitable societies in the world, blacks and mulattos still did not gain political power commensurate with their increasing importance in Cuban society. The revolutionary leadership, with a few notable exceptions that proved the rule, remained predominantly white and male. In 1986 the Communist party of Cuba publicly acknowledged that Cubans of color were underrepresented in party and government leadership positions. The party called for the promotion of blacks to positions of leadership. The official explanation for the shortcomings was surprisingly honest: "It is not enough to establish laws on equality and expect total equality. It has to be promoted in mass organizations, in party youth. . . . We cannot expect women, blacks, mixed-race people to be promoted spontaneously."

Racial attitudes and discriminatory practices are resistant to change, even in revolutionary Cuba. Law and custom may now make it impossible to discriminate against Cubans of color, but Cubans still hold racial prejudices. It is not uncommon to hear Cubans on the street complain about the overwhelming tendencies of blacks to engage in crime. And while interracial unions are more common today than in the past, it is not true that Cubans do not make any racial distinctions. Indeed, they use many racial categories to identify people. A dark-skinned Cuban may be regarded simply as a *negro*, but there are many finer distinctions defining persons of mixed racial heritage, such as *pardo, moreno,* or *indio.* For a revolution that has been determined to portray itself as nonracial, the Cubans remain deeply aware of and divided by race.

The revolutionary government, primarily through the Ministry of Culture, has used race and culture to promote national political objectives and a new national identity. The government shifted the cultural focus from forms that reflected elite interests, such as ballet, to ideas, images, and activities that reflected the revolution's commitment to social equality and justice. Thus, the Ministry of Culture has actively promoted Afro-Cuban rumba as a national dance. Rumba had developed in the mid-nineteenth century among poor free black communities, particularly in Havana. By the 1930s, its popularity had spread across the island and to the United States and Europe, one of several music dance crazes emanating from Cuba. According to anthropologist Yvonne Daniel, the Ministry of Culture decided after 1959 that "rumba, apparently more than other Cuban dance traditions, expressed an identification with African-derived elements that make up Cuban culture, represented the interests of workers, and solidified the participation of the Cuban artistic community in the social advance of the new political system."

For similar reasons, the government created a state-sponsored troupe in 1962 to support Afro-Cuban performances of the Santería religion. By elevating Santería from a secretive and mysterious religious sect to a national folkloric tradition, the government demonstrated its support for racial and social equality. The troupe has made Santería a more "acceptable" religious and cultural expression by presenting spectacular performances of Afro-Cuban rituals. At the same time, these government-controlled performances present a stylized version of Santería for popular consumption that are increasingly unlike actual rituals, particularly when they are presented at tourist hotels for foreign visitors. Some Afro-Cuban groups have complained that these highly choreographed and dramatized shows "trivialize the importance of the Afro-Cuban contribution to Cuba's national cultural heritage," according to ethnomusicologist Katherine J. Hagedorn.

The institutionalization of the revolution undoubtedly opened up opportunities for Cubans of color. In 1961 the government created a National Institute for Sports, Physical Education, and Recreation (INDER) to promote physical education and competitive athletics at every level of every sport. With the responsibility for selecting and developing the best athletes, INDER operates training facilities and teams throughout the island. Gifted athletes receive government grants to pursue their athletic careers under the guidance of the nation's best trainers. Such support was not generally available to poor black Cubans before 1959, but thanks to the revolution's emphasis on mass participation in athletics, black Cubans have contributed greatly to Cuba's superb record in the Olympic and Pan-American games. Teofilo Stevenson won three consecutive Olympic gold medals in boxing, thanks in no small part to an ambitious government program that gave him the opportunity to develop his natural skills. After his retirement, Stevenson, a loyal supporter of the revolution, was elected to the Central Committee of the Communist party in 1991.

While black Cubans have gained international fame as athletes, musicians, writers, and artists, few of them have reached the highest positions of political power in the government. Today, forty-seven years after the Cuban revolution supposedly suppressed racial discrimination, blacks are still underrepresented in the party and government. Of the twenty-five members of the Political Bureau of the Communist party in 2004, only four persons were black; of the thirty-nine members of the Council of Ministers, only two were black; and of the fourteen presidents of the provincial assemblies, only one was black. Yet at least 40 percent of Cubans on an island of nearly 11 million people are identified as black or mulatto. Thus, while the Cuban revolution has trained record numbers of Afro-Cuban doctors, lawyers, engineers, and administrators, there are still some racial barriers that block their climb to the highest levels of political authority in revolutionary Cuba. In a government that controls the expression of Afro-Cuban identity in music and religion, the absence of black Cubans in the highest ranks of government has allowed white Cubans to define black culture.

WOMEN IN REVOLUTIONARY CUBA

Women played decisive roles during the fight against Batista as well as the construction of socialism after 1959. Two women, Melba Hernández and Haydée Santamaría, participated in the Moncada assault on July 26, 1953. They served in the unit led by Abel Santamaría, Haydée's brother, which took over the hospital adjacent to the barracks. In the horrifying aftermath of the failed attack, Batista's soldiers captured Melba and Haydée and took them to Moncada, where they witnessed the torture of several fidelistas, including Abel and Boris Luís Santa Coloma, Haydée's fiancée. The Batista regime treated men and women with near equal brutality, a fact that explains why so many women joined the 26th of July Movement and served as organizers, fundraisers, couriers, diplomats, and combatants.

Melba and Haydée subsequently assumed leadership roles on the directorate of the 26th of July Movement, spending some time in the Sierra Maestra alongside Celia Sánchez and Vílma Espín, the most powerful women in the organization. Celia, the daughter of a doctor who lived in Manzanillo, organized the clandestine organization that kept the *Granma* survivors alive after the disastrous battle of Alegría del Pío. Without the money, supplies, and recruits that Celia's support network provided to the rebel army, it is doubtful that the fidelistas would have managed to reorganize in the Sierra Maestra. After her position in Manzanillo became too dangerous, she joined Castro in the Sierra Maestra and became Fidel's closest associate. Unmarried and completely devoted to Fidel and the revolution, she became, in the words of Castro biographer Tad Szulc, "the most important woman—and very likely the most important human being—in his life."

At Castro's side in the La Plata headquarters, she functioned as Fidel's de facto chief of staff, a role she played until her death in 1980. In Havana, Celia's small apartment in Vedado became a home, refuge, and office for Fidel, who often slept there. To gain access to Fidel one often had to go through Celia, the semi-official gatekeeper of the revolution. Though loyal and devoted to Fidel, "she was probably the only one in Cuba to tell him to his face that he was making a bad decision, although she told others that 'Fidel is always right,'" Szulc explains.

Vílma Espín, who studied engineering at the Massachusetts Institute of Technology before joining Raúl Castro's rebel column in the Sierra Maestra, assumed a formal position of power after Fidel gained power. She married Raúl in 1959 and established herself as a political force as the founding president of the Cuban Women's Federation (FMC). Organized in 1961 with an initial membership of 17,000, the FMC became a powerful voice for women within the revolutionary movement. By 1985, membership in the FMC had grown to 2.6 million, representing 82 percent of all women over the age of fourteen. Espín's influence grew as well. She became a full member of the Political Bureau of the Communist party in 1986, the only woman to serve on this powerful body.

The powerful women who served the Cuban revolution placed the highest priority on the revolution, not gender equity. As in the case of racial issues, general issues of sexual discrimination took a back seat to the larger struggle against capitalism and imperialism. The revolutionaries certainly recognized gender discrimination as a problem and supported legislation that has made remarkable progress in a notoriously sexist society. Even the men who welcomed women into the ranks of the rebel army wanted to limit their activities to the supportive roles typically assigned to females: caring for the wounded, preparing meals, and even ironing the clothes of the combatants. The fact that the most powerful women in the organization were attached to important male leaders (Celia and Fidel, Vílma and Raúl, Haydée and Armando Hart) suggests there were some limits to female opportunities. These women understood the social realities of the day. Cuban men, on the left and right wings of the political spectrum, displayed little tolerance for women in positions of political authority. The Cuban political system, buttressed by strongly chauvinistic attitudes, offered few opportunities for women to advance politically, economically, or socially.

The women who served in the July 26th Movement, however, used the power they attained through the revolution to advance the cause of women's liberation, gender equity, and social justice. Women mobilized to promote and defend the revolution in its earliest days. And women figured prominently in the ranks of the literacy brigades in 1961. They joined the militias and the Committees for the Defense of the Revolution, serving alongside men in the efforts to combat the counter-revolutionary threat. Women also served in the volunteer work brigades, cutting sugar cane just like men in the national effort to harvest the failed goal of 10 million tons of sugar. The result of these mobilizations transformed women and, ultimately, the nature of the revolution. Historian Lou Pérez explains: "Women who had previously never worked outside the home traveled across the interior countryside as teachers, agricultural workers, and administrators. For many, it was their first experience in positions previously reserved for men, in the factories, in the fields, on construction sites, as operators of machinery, and as managers of state enterprises."

Women benefited from the egalitarian objectives of the revolutionary program. They took full advantage of the educational opportunities afforded by the revolution to enter careers that previously lay beyond their reach. By 1995, 48 percent of all physicians in Cuba were women. Women entered every sector of the workforce in record numbers. In pre-1959 Cuba, women represented only 15 percent of the total workforce; by 1995, women accounted for nearly 41 percent of it. With salaries and wages tightly controlled by the government, there is little disparity between men and women. According to the 1995 Human Development Report of the United Nations Development Program, Cuba "leads the developing world in gender equality."

The entry of so many women in the workforce initially created greater burdens on Cuban women, as many now found themselves working a "triple shift": they worked at a factory during the day, attended political meetings in the early evening, and took care of their homes and children at all other times. Cuban men might not have objected to the incorporation of women into the workforce, but their values still held women back at home. Many husbands refused to share the burdens of home and childcare with their wives, leading the FMC to demand legislation to share responsibilities at home. The result was the passage of the Family Code in 1974. In addition to providing equal job opportunities without regard to gender, the Family Code also established the principle that both husbands and wives enjoyed the right to pursue their careers and improve their education. The code made men equally responsible for the maintenance of the home and the upbringing of the children.

Despite such relatively progressive legislation, women have had difficulty changing the patriarchal attitudes of men, most of whom perceived the Family Code as a lofty statement of theory, not a practical reality. Men often paid lip service to the goal of women's liberation without changing their personal behavior. While women entered the workforce at levels unparalleled in the Western Hemisphere, they still encountered the same glass ceiling that obstructs women's promotion in capitalist societies. Women were generally underrepresented at supervisory and executive levels of state enterprises. The under-representation of women at the highest levels of the Communist party and the government is perhaps the most telling critique of the revolution's contributions to women's liberation. Only two of the twenty-five members of the Politburo in 2004 were women; only six of the thirty-nine members of the Council of Ministers were women; and none of the fourteen Provincial Assembly presidents was a woman.

While Cuba has made significant gains in terms of gender equity, most notably in levels of employment and education, the progress of women in revolutionary Cuba presents a unique paradox. According to feminist scholar Marisela Fleites-Lear, women gained the freedom to join the political and social movement of the revolution, but this same freedom doubled or even tripled their workloads. While women gained more sexual freedom, their relationships became unstable as women challenged traditional patterns of behavior. Divorce rates have increased partly as a result. Women gained more political power than ever before, but they could not organize institutions or promote policies without the express authorization of institutions dominated by males. Cuban men, therefore, have retained the power to define the political agenda for women. As one might expect, the male leaders placed a higher priority on issues of class conflict and the general struggle against imperialism than issues such as gender equity in government positions or equal pay for equal work. The FMC, dominated by female leaders completely loyal to the revolution, has only been able to work for change within a system whose limits are defined by male authorities.

Hence, the primary value of the FMC to Fidel Castro and the revolutionary leadership is as a means of mobilizing and controlling the female population. It is a powerful organization lacking in political autonomy, as is the case with other social and political organizations in revolutionary Cuba. It does not provide an open forum for women to express their grievances about progressive legislation that is rarely enforced. Cuban women have made tremendous strides in the struggle for sexual equality, yet sexist images and language remain pervasive. "Despite the positive aspects of these achievements, thirty-six years of Revolution have not lead to a truly egalitarian society," Fleites-Lear explains. "Cuba remains, at its core, a patriarchal society."

THE SPECIAL PERIOD, 1990–2005

The severe and prolonged economic crisis into which Cuba plunged in the early 1990s threatened all the progress made in race and gender relations since 1959. The crisis, in fact, threatened the very existence of the Cuban revolution and its maximum leader, Fidel Castro. The economic foundations of the institutional revolution collapsed with the disintegration of the Soviet Union and its communist bloc allies. Foreign observers, particularly Cuban Americans in the United States, predicted the imminent demise or overthrow of Fidel Castro, convinced that Cuba could not possibly withstand the loss of $3 billion worth of annual subsidies. Yet Castro and the Cuban revolution survived, despite mounting economic hardships for the average Cuban, male or female, black or white.

Castro was well prepared to weather the economic crisis. In 1986, the government had initiated a campaign designed to moderate the course of the Soviet-style development program that had been implemented in the early 1970s. The Cuban revolutionaries felt that they had overemphasized the individual over the community, the material over the moral incentives. Determined to correct these errors, the government launched a "rectification" campaign that it promoted as a return to the revolutionary idealism of the 1960s. Once again the government called on workers to sacrifice their individual interests for the benefit of the nation. The mini-brigades of "volunteer" workers reappeared to build homes, day care centers, and cut sugar cane.

Castro felt that workers, both high and low, had lost some of their revolutionary fervor and dedication. High-ranking officers in the military and security services, including General Arnaldo Ochoa and Colonel Antonio de la Guardia, had allegedly abused the privileges of their rank to travel and acquire luxury items not available to the average consumer. In 1989, the government tried Ochoa, de la Guardia, and other prominent officials on charges of trafficking in drugs and betraying the Cuban revolution. General Ochoa, former commander of Cuban forces in Ethiopia and Angola, was a legitimate hero of the Cuban revolution. For some reason he fell out of favor with Castro, who personally presented the case against Ochoa in the courtroom. The case fueled speculation that Castro considered Ochoa, a popular and charismatic man with a loyal following in the army, a dangerous political rival. Castro denied any political motivations behind the charges, but Cubans knew that Ochoa's conviction was a foregone conclusion. They were nevertheless surprised by the execution of Ochoa, de la Guardia, and two other men at dawn on July 13, 1989. Never in the history of the Cuban Revolution had such high-ranking revolutionary officers been brought before a firing squad. Castro was not in a compromising mood, and he wanted to send a message.

Over the next few weeks, Castro carried out a purge that included the dismissal of the powerful minister of the interior, Division General José Abrantes, and dozens of top military and civilian officers. The executions, coming less than four months after Gorbachev's visit to Havana, sent a clear message to all internal dissidents and foreign enemies that Cuba would not tolerate change. "After what had happened in Eastern Europe," journalist Andres Oppenheimer explains, Castro "was determined not to allow a political opening in Cuba that could develop into a full-blown revolution."

Accordingly, Castro's answer to the economic crisis of the early 1990s was retrenchment, not reform. There would be no national debate about the virtues of democracy and free market reform; the one-party state was not open for discussion, at least not in public forums. Change could only come from within the existing revolutionary system. Thus, in August 1990, Castro declared a "Special Period in Time of Peace," and called on the Cuban people to make exceptional sacrifices for the duration of the crisis. Over the next few years, the government acted as if Cuba were in a state of war, implementing a series of austerity measures and economic reforms designed to ensure the survival of the revolution.

The most pressing need was to earn foreign exchange, meaning dollars. The Soviets—and the Russians after them—demanded that trade be conducted in dollars, forcing the Cubans to seek dollars on the international market. One means of getting foreign exchange into Cuba was to attract more foreign tourists and require them to spend U.S. dollars. The government actively promoted the expansion of tourism by allowing foreign investment, primarily as joint ventures. Within a few years, foreign companies had invested in luxury hotels in Havana and Varadero Beach. Promotional campaigns lured foreign tourists to the island, still famed for its pristine beaches, lively culture, and beautiful women. Tourism leaped from 350,000 visitors in 1990 to 600,000 in 1993. By 1994, tourism generated more than $500 million in revenue, making it the most valuable sector of the Cuban economy.

In August 1993, the government went a step further in its efforts to acquire dollars when it legalized the U.S. dollar as the currency of exchange. Prior to this time, it was a crime for any Cuban citizen to hold U.S. dollars. Cubans had dollars, nonetheless, and they used them to purchase food and goods on a flourishing black market. Friends and relatives in the United States, increasingly concerned about the health of their loved ones in Cuba, sent money whenever possible or took clothes, pharmaceuticals, and other badly needed products with them on annual visits allowed by the United States. By legalizing the use of the dollar, the Cuban government hoped to increase the flow of dollar remittances from the United States and divert these dollars into the formal economy, where they could be used to pay its debts and purchase products on the international market. As anticipated, the value of remittances from the United States to Cuba increased in the 1990s, with some estimates as high as $1 billion annually.

The influx of dollars provided a lift to the economy and encouraged a limited experiment with free-market reforms. Farmers' markets reappeared, allowing growers to sell surplus production at market prices. State enterprises were given greater autonomy and ordered to increase productivity and show a profit. The government once again allowed self-employment in a few occupations. The ever-creative and hard working Cuban people responded by opening hair salons, auto repair shops, and even some small private restaurants. The government authorized people to open private restaurants in their homes to serve tourists as well as locals. The restaurants, known as *paladares*, had to be licensed by the state and pay taxes in dollars. Seating capacity was strictly limited, and advertising was prohibited, but for a few years the paladares offered the best food at reasonable prices, primarily in Havana.

The economy responded slowly. After several years of reduced rations and electrical shortages and rolling blackouts, the Cuban economy began to recover. Foreign companies responded to the economic opportunities offered by the Cuban government, which included tax exemptions and guarantees regarding the freedom to repatriate profits. The highly educated and disciplined labor force, combined with the relative absence of crime and a relatively stable society, made Cuba one of the most attractive countries in the developing world. The number of foreign companies operating in Cuba increased from one hundred in 1987 to five hundred in 1994, with joint ventures in mining, construction, hotels, transportation, utilities, and pharmaceuticals.

The desperate measures taken by the government led many observers to question the credibility of a government committed to an egalitarian society. Cubans chafe at the reappearance of foreign hotels in which European and North American tourists enjoy accommodations and luxuries unknown to most Cubans; the resort hotels are, in fact, off-limits to the Cubans. They might bribe their way into the lobby bar, but they may not accompany a foreign tourist into a hotel room upstairs. These rules have had little negative impact on prostitution, which reappeared in force, thirty years after the government claimed to have eliminated it. Many urban women, including doctors, nurses, engineers, and lawyers, have elected to supplement their meager income of $15 per month by offering themselves to the foreign tourists. Castro, unwilling to admit the existence of the poor social conditions that have adversely affected women's lives, denies that these women serve as prostitutes. He labeled these hustlers *jineteras* (jockeys), women who are now engaged in a new form of prostitution. The jineteras make their way into the tourist hotels to charm a foreign visitor. They do not ask for cash in exchange for sex, but they certainly expect compensation for it after a delightful evening in bars and restaurants that only accept dollars.

The development of tourism has also had a negative impact on race relations and the struggle to eliminate discrimination. Indeed, some observers have noted a dangerous resurgence of racial discrimination and a general racial imbalance during the Special Period. Foreign hotel companies, for example, are reluctant to hire dark-skinned Cubans because foreign tourists supposedly want to be served by whites. Moreover, because black Cubans have fewer friends and relatives in the United States, they do not generally receive the large cash remittances that have kept white Cuban families afloat for years. The result is that the Special Period Reforms have exacerbated differences between the races and threaten to undo whatever gains have been made.

Cuba's economic recovery has been all the more remarkable when one considers the measures adopted by the United States to try to worsen the hardships Cubans must endure. In 1992, Republican President George H. W. Bush tightened the economic embargo by approving the Torricelli Act. The legislation, endorsed by the powerful Cuban American National Foundation (CANF) based in Miami, prohibited subsidiaries of American companies in other countries from trading with Cuba. In 1996, Democratic President Bill Clinton tightened the screws even further by passing the Cuban Liberty and Democratic Solidarity Act, also known as the Helms-Burton Act. This act, supported by the CANF but opposed by every major American ally, authorized American citizens to sue foreign companies that traded with or invested in Cuban companies that possessed properties expropriated by Castro after 1959. Although Clinton initially opposed the legislation, he approved it in March 1996, just a few weeks after Cuban planes shot down two U.S. civilian planes, killing four Cuban American members of a relief organization known as Brothers to the Rescue. The outrage in the Cuban American community led Clinton to sign Helms-Burton during a presidential election year, a sign that both Democrats and Republicans recognized the electoral power of Cuban Americans in south Florida. Because of strong opposition from European countries, Clinton and his successor, President George W. Bush, have not enforced the part of the law that allows U.S. citizens to sue foreign companies.

Strengthening the American embargo against Cuba has not weakened Fidel Castro's hold on the nation. There is no indication that his power—or that of the Communist party—is slipping. Although there are frequent reminders that many Cubans would rather die trying to cross the Straits of Florida on a raft than remain in Cuba, there is little likelihood of a domestic rebellion. Castro's militant opponents, such as Delta 66, operate in south Florida, and hardly have the capacity to present a serious military challenge to Cuba. The political reality is that Fidel survived the collapse of the Soviet Union, the U.S. embargo, and the administrations of ten American presidents.

And Castro has used the continuing struggle against the United States to rally the Cuban people behind a nationalist crusade. On many different occasions since 1959, he skillfully exploited the United States to gain political advantage at home. During the political and legal struggle over Elián González, an eight-year-old Cuban boy rescued at sea in 2000 after an ill-fated attempt to defect from Cuba on an unseaworthy raft, Castro denounced the United States and the Cuban American community for denying the father's request to have the boy returned to him in Cuba. Relatives of the boy's mother, who died when the raft capsized, wanted to keep the boy in Miami. After months of demonstrations in Havana and Miami, federal authorities seized Elián in a stunning raid of his relatives' home in April 2000 and returned him to his father.

In this and so many other psychological and diplomatic battles with the United States and the Cuban exile community, Castro has always prevailed. He used the Elián González case to strengthen his political position at home, just as he uses the American embargo to explain economic shortages in Cuba. His survival and that of the revolution is not due, however, to American policy, and his downfall, whenever it comes, is more likely to come from internal opponents or natural causes than any action initiated by the United States. Cubans, whether in Miami or Santa Clara, are fierce and determined nationalists who resist any foreign interference in their internal affairs. Castro has escaped several assassination attempts in the early 1960s and the Cuban Revolution has survived a severe economic depression in the early 1990s. Castro remains committed to the defense of the socialist revolution, perhaps the last revolutionary in the world. He typically ends his speeches—which sometimes go on for hours these days, the elderly man sometimes rambling—with a call to arms: "Socialism or Death!" His critics respond: "Socialism is Death!"

❧ Conclusion ❧

"*F*or suffering Cuba, the first word." These words of José Martí, spoken over one hundred years ago, would still call Cubans to attention today. Whether in Miami, Havana, Tampa, or Santiago, Cubans still pay homage to the apostle of Cuban liberty and his dream of Cuba Libre, the ideal republic based on the highest standards of justice, morality, democracy, and equality.

Cubans on both sides of the Florida Straits would readily acknowledge that the state of their beloved country remains far from their cherished ideal. Many Cuban Americans in the United States, those for and against the embargo, fear that they will not live to see their highest ambitions fulfilled. Cubans on the island, revolutionaries as well as dissidents, would have to admit that the revolution has not created a workers paradise. Thousands of them attempt to escape Castro's Cuba every year, dreaming of a better life in the United States. Cubans differ on the causes of their shortcomings, the means to their desired end, and perhaps even the end itself, but the goal of redeeming the nation and their willingness to sacrifice for it still unites them.

Anybody who has witnessed Cuban American political demonstrations in Miami understands the passion that Cubans feel for the cause of national liberation. Cubans on the island are no less passionate about their homeland, even though many would welcome the opportunity to leave it. Yet many more stay, enduring political and economic hardships that few Americans could possibly understand. Some would even prefer imprisonment on the island to freedom on the United States mainland.

Sadly, Cuba still suffers. Visitors to the island often wonder how the Cuban people can endure such deprivation. They ask why they do not fight against the dictatorship or die in the effort. They doubt that the revolution can survive much longer, but there are few signs, other than Castro's declining health, that the regime is faltering. Most of all, they dream of what Cuba will be like after Castro is gone. They envision the opportunities that will come with freedom, the right to rebuild their homes and businesses, to recreate the Cuba that was. Residents of the island await the opportunity to earn more money and buy American consumer goods. But they also hope that they can maintain some of the social achievements of the revolution, such as universal health care and education.

Nobody can predict when Castro will die or how he might be removed from power. Raúl Castro is the official successor to Fidel, but few people envisage the revolution living long past him. Cuban Americans cannot imagine that after the regime Cubans on the island—after forty-seven years of economic stagnation and political repression—will fail to embrace democracy and free enterprise. The poor and disadvantaged Cubans who benefited from the revolution, however, are not so eager to discard Castro and embrace the Miami Cubans, whom they associate with the repression of the Batista regime. The future of post-Castro Cuba depends on the interaction of revolutionaries and anti-communists who have little common political ground beyond a shared reverence for Martí and his vision of the ideal republic.

The future of Cuba hinges on many factors over which no prognosticator has control, such as the means by which Fidel is removed from power. Old age may get to him before an assassin, but it is still possible that a military coup sponsored by Cuban dissidents may terminate the revolution. Yet Fidel Castro did not make the revolution by himself, and the fact is that the revolution may outlive him. There are currently 500,000 members of the Communist party in Cuba, and they may not surrender power so quickly or easily. Moreover, officers loyal to Raúl Castro command the armed forces, and they may not capitulate without a negotiated agreement.

It is possible that the future of Cuba may look much like the past, full of broken dreams, political rebellions, economic dependency, social injustice, and inspirational orators who claim to know what to do about these conditions. History weighs heavily on Cuban political culture. The political ideal to which they aspire is, perhaps, a utopian vision of a republic that can never be created. The ideal republic will always be a work in progress, not an accomplished feat.

Yet Cubans demand change from Cuban and American leaders. These leaders, however, refuse to engage in a reasonable dialogue across the waters because of their pride, economic interests, personal animosity, political necessity, and more. They are right to point out that all previous attempts at negotiation have failed. They are right to point out that Fidel Castro will only leave

Cuba in a coffin. And while people in high office on both sides of the Florida Straits maintain a strict silence on the future of Cuba, children go without food and are separated from their parents, political dissidents waste away in jails, and senior citizens long for the Cuba of their childhood.

The cause of Cuba Libre still commands attention. There are deep, probably irreconcilable, political differences among the Cuban people that make a negotiated political solution difficult if not impossible. In Cuban political culture, on the island and in south Florida, before and after the revolution, compromise is an aberration, not the norm. Principles are not negotiated; honor is defended to the death. The culture values and exalts those who have refused to compromise in their struggle to defend the country. Exemplary death in service of the country has been a tradition of Cuban patriots since the late nineteenth century. Carlos Manuel de Céspedes, the father of the Cuban nation, called on Cubans to triumph or die in the fight against Spain, and he demonstrated his commitment to the cause by dying on the battlefield with an empty revolver. Calixto García, one of his leading military commanders, attempted suicide rather than accept the dishonor associated with surrender. These and many other acts of self-sacrifice have been so ennobled that death in service of the country is expected of Cuban leaders. Martyrdom is even sanctified in the Cuban national anthem, which includes the line, "to die for the patria is to live."

Given this national political culture, one should not be surprised to learn that Cuba has long had one of the highest rates of suicide in the world. Suicide, rather than an irrational and immoral act, is considered a rational, normal response to an unacceptable life. There is a peculiar Cuban "way of death," as historian Louis Pérez explains. "The gesture of self-immolation," he argues, "has become so commonly associated with upholding the ideals of nationality as to pass easily enough for a virtue of [being] Cuban." History provides too many examples of Cuban patriots who preferred death to life with dishonor.

But martyrdom is, unfortunately, a recurrent theme in Cuban history, while political compromise and civil discourse have not been. In the six decades before Fidel Castro, Cubans made little progress toward their goal of creating the ideal republic. Political corruption and violence were endemic; elections were often fraudulent or simply ignored. Cuba was poor and prosperous, beautiful and unattractive. The land was hardly a utopia before Castro, and it will not be one after him. The death or removal of Castro will not necessarily solve Cuba's problems and lead to the creation of a prosperous democratic nation. Perhaps Cubans will settle for a modest amount of democracy and prosperity in a peaceful and orderly society that will always struggle to create *Cuba Libre*.

❧ Bibliographical Essay ❧

*T*here are several general surveys that cover the history of Cuba from colonial times through the revolution. The starting point for any review of Cuban history is Louis A. Pérez, Jr., *Cuba: Between Reform and Revolution*, 3d ed. (2006). Broader in scope and written from a different political perspective is the monumental work of Hugh Thomas, *Cuba: The Pursuit of Freedom* (1971). There are several concise histories of Cuba, including Jaime Suchlicki, *Cuba: From Columbus to Castro*, 2d ed. (1986), Clifford L. Staten, *The History of Cuba* (2003), and Richard Gott, *Cuba: A New History* (2004). Leslie Bethell, ed., *Cuba: A Short History* (1993) contains brief essays by academic experts in various fields. Aviva Chomsky and Barry Carr, eds., *The Cuba Reader: History, Culture, Politics* (2003), is a valuable compilation of documents and articles covering Cuban history from European contact to the present.

Those who can read Spanish will benefit from numerous works in Cuban history written by Cuban specialists. An indispensable reference work on Cuban study is the ten-volume history compiled by Ramiro Guerra y Sánchez, *Historia de la nación cubana* (1952). Although dated, it is a comprehensive account of Cuban history written by a team of experts. A more recent but equally ambitious work is another collaborative effort led by Levi Marrero, *Cuba, economía y sociedad*, 15 vols. (1972–88). For briefer works written by Cuban historians see Emilio Roig de Leuchsenring, *Curso de introducción a la historia de Cuba* (1938), and Carlos Márquez Sterling and Manuel Márquez Sterling, *Historia de la isla de Cuba* (1975). For a historical survey written after the revolution see Julio LeRiverend, *Breve historia de Cuba* (1981). One must understand the history of sugar to understand the history of Cuba, and there has been no greater contribution to the field than the three-volume work by

Cuban historian Manuel Moreno Fraginals, *El ingenio: complejo económico-social cubano del azúcar* (Havana, 1978). On the history of twentieth-century Cuba, with particular emphasis on the revolution, see Marifeli Pérez-Stable, *The Cuban Revolution: Origins, Course, and Legacy,* 2d ed. (1999). One can learn more about twentieth-century Cuba · through the biographies of Fidel Castro. Of these, the most complete and reliable are Tad Szulc, *Fidel: A Critical Portrait* (1986), and Robert Quirk, *Fidel Castro* (1993). For a general overview of United States relations with Cuba see Louis A. Pérez, Jr., *Cuba and the United States: Ties of Singular Intimacy* (1990).

CHAPTER ONE:
THE KEY TO THE NEW WORLD, 1492–1825

For a brief overview of the pre-Columbian Taíno civilization, see Irving Rouse, *The Taínos: Rise & Decline of the People who Greeted Columbus* (1992). A more comprehensive study of Cuba prior to the arrival of the Europeans is Ernest E. Tabio and Estrella Rey, *Prehistoria de Cuba* (1966).

A good starting point for a study of European contact, exploration, and conquest of Cuba is Samuel Elliot Morison, *The European Discovery of America: The Southern Voyages, 1492–1619* (1974), and his two-volume biography, *Admiral of the Ocean Sea: A Life of the Admiral Christopher Columbus* (1942). For the classic denunciation of the conquest, see the accounts of an eyewitness, Bartolome de las Casas, *The Devastation of the Indies: A Brief Account*, translated by Herma Briffault (1992). For a highly critical interpretation of Columbus and the Spanish conquistadors consult Kirkpatrick Sale, *The Conquest of Paradise: Christopher Columbus and the Columbian Legacy* (1990) and David Stannard, *American Holocaust: Columbus and the Conquest of the New World* (1992).

One can also glean early Cuban history from general accounts of Spanish explorations and conquest such as Arthur Percival Newton, *The European Nations in the West Indies, 1493–1688* (1967); Troy S. Floyd, *The Columbus Dynasty in the Caribbean, 1492–1526* (1973); and Carl Sauer, *The Early Spanish Main* (1966). To go beyond the military and political aspects of the encounter see Alfred Cosby, Jr., *The Colombian Exchange: Biological and Cultural Consequences of 1492* (1972).

On the early history of Cuba, works in English are scarce. Irene Wright, *The Early History of Cuba, 1492–1586* (1916), has yet to be surpassed. Wright extends her work in two articles, "Rescates: With Special Reference to Cuba,

1599–1610," *Hispanic American Historical Review* 3 (August 1920): 333–61; and "The Dutch and Cuba, 1609–1643," *Hispanic American Historical Review* 9 (November 1921): 597–634.

The literature on international rivalries and warfare in the colonial Caribbean is rich. Kenneth R. Andrews, *The Spanish Caribbean: Trade and Plunder, 1530–1630* (1978) examines Spanish conflict with the French, English, and Dutch in the region. On the buccaneers of the seventeenth century see Clarence Haring, *The Buccaneers in the West Indies in the XVII Century* (1916), a dated but valuable work. The classic history of the British assault on Havana during the Seven Years' War is Francis Russell Hart, *The Siege of Havana* (1931).

For specialized studies of colonial Cuba in the eighteenth and nineteenth centuries see Maria Elena Diaz, *The Virgin, the King, and the Royal Slaves of El Cobre: Negotiating Freedom in Colonial Cuba, 1670–1780* (2001); Sherry Johnson, *The Social Transformation of 18th Century Cuba* (2001); Allan J. Kuethe, *Cuba, 1753–1815: Crown, Military, and Society* (1986); and Kenneth Kiple, *Blacks in Colonial Cuba, 1774–1899* (1976). On the development of Cuba's two most important crops in the colonial era, the standard is Fernando Ortiz, *Cuban Counterpoint: Tobacco and Sugar* (1947).

Chapter Two:
The Wars for Independence, 1825–1898

There are a number of excellent studies of slavery and its abolition in the nineteenth century. The old standard, Hubert Aimes, *A History of Slavery in Cuba, 1511–1868* (1907), is still valuable, as is the work by respected Cuban historian Fernando Ortiz, *Los esclavos negros* (1916). Franklin Knight's *Slave Society in Cuba during the Nineteenth Century* (1970) examines the social and economic aspects of Cuban slavery, and Herbert S. Klein, *Slavery in the Americas: A Comparative Study of Cuba and Virginia* (1967), attempts to place Cuban slavery in a broader perspective. On the international efforts to suppress the African slave trade see David Murray, *Odious Commerce: Britain, Spain, and the Abolition of the Cuban Slave Trade* (1980). Rebecca Scott tells the complete story of abolition in *Slave Emancipation in Cuba* (1985). For a detailed study of the 1844 rebellion see Robert Paquette, *Sugar is Made with Blood: The Conspiracy of La Escalera and the Conflict between Empires over Slavery in Cuba* (1988). The social and economic history of the sugar industry in central Cuba is covered in Laird Bergad, *Cuban Rural Society in the Nineteenth Century: The Social and Economic History of Monoculture in Matanzas* (1990).

The literature on the wars for independence is voluminous. Cuban historians have traditionally focused on the patriotic leaders and their heroic campaigns over a thirty-year period, while their American counterparts have focused on the brief military campaign of 1898. Americans tend to ignore the duration and severity of the struggle, but that oversight can be remedied by consulting a number of excellent works by Cuban historians, beginning with Ramiro Guerra y Sánchez, *Guerra de los diez años, 1868–1878* (1972). On the critical period between the wars, see Louis A. Pérez, Jr., *Cuba between Empires, 1878–1902* (1983). Gerald Poyo explores the history of the Cuban exile communities in the United States and their contributions to independence in *"With All, and for the Good of All": The Emergence of Popular Nationalism in the Cuban Communities of the United States, 1848–1898* (1989). Ada Ferrer, *Insurgent Cuba: Race, Nation, and Revolution, 1868–1898* (1999), analyzes the struggles of Cuban patriots to define the place of persons of color within the boundaries of Cuban nationalism. Joan Casanovas, *Urban Labor and Spanish Colonialism in Cuba, 1850–1898* (1998) also sheds light on the independence movement.

The most comprehensive work in English on the war for independence is the two-volume work of Philip Foner, *The Spanish-Cuban-American War and the Birth of American Imperialism* (1972). Foner echoes the arguments of Cuban historian Emilio Roig de Leuchsenring, who argues that the Cubans were on the verge of victory when the Americans intervened in *Cuba no debe su independencia a los Estados Unidos,* 3d ed. (1960). It is now a standard tenet of Cuban historiography that the Cuban Army of Liberation had virtually defeated the Spanish prior to the American intervention. American historians nonetheless emphasize American contributions to Cuban independence by confounding the Cuban War for Independence with the Spanish-American War. For a sampling of American treatment of the military campaign of 1898 see the pictorial history of Frank Freidel, *The Splendid Little War* (1958); Ivan Musicant, *Empire by Default: The Spanish-American War and the Dawn of the American Century* (1998); and George O'Toole, *The Spanish War, an American Epic—1898* (1984). Louis A. Pérez, Jr., surveys the historiography of the war in *The War of 1898: The United States and Cuba in History and Historiography* (1998).

One can also look at the history of nineteenth-century Cuba and the wars for independence through the biographies and memoirs of its leaders. Jorge Mañach's *Martí: Apostle of Freedom* (1950) is a well written and laudatory account that reflects the traditional image of Martí in Cuban historiography. For more objective treatments of Martí see John M. Kirk, *José Martí: Mentor of the Cuban Nation* (1983). Martí's own writings also provide insight into his political philosophy and Cuban history. See Philip Foner, ed., *Inside the Monster: Writings on the United States and American Imperialism* (1975) and *Our America: Writings on Latin America and the Struggle for Cuban Independence* (1977). Foner also published the standard biography of Maceo in English, *Antonio Maceo: The 'Bronze Titan' of Cuba's Struggle for Independence* (1977).

CHAPTER THREE:
THE FIRST REPUBLIC, 1898–1934

For a history of the American occupation see David F. Healy, *The United States in Cuba, 1898–1902* (1963). The second volume of Philip Foner's *The Spanish-Cuban-American War and the Birth of American Imperialism, 1895–1902* (1972) also covers these critical years. Allan Reed Millett covers the second American occupation in *The Politics of Intervention: The Military Occupation of Cuba, 1906–1909* (1968). For a broader examination of American relations with Cuba during the First Republic see two books by Louis A. Pérez, Jr., *Cuba Under the Platt Amendment, 1902–1934* (1986) and *Intervention, Revolution, and Politics in Cuba, 1913–1921* (1978). Other valuable analyses of United States relations with Cuba under the Platt Amendment include José M. Hernández, *Cuba and the United States: Intervention and Militarism, 1868–1933* (1993); and Jules Robert Benjamin *The United States and Cuba: Hegemony and Dependent Development, 1880–1934* (1977).

For a narrative of political turmoil during the First Republic see the old history by Charles Chapman, *A History of the Cuban Republic* (1927). On American economic interests in Cuba see the classic by Leland Jenks, *Our Cuban Colony* (1928). For a standard study of the sugar industry see Ramiro Guerra y Sánchez, *Sugar and Society in the Caribbean* (1964). Aline Helg covers the events leading to the 1912 rebellion in *Our Rightful Share: The Afro-Cuban Struggle for Equality, 1886–1912* (1995). Louis A. Pérez, Jr., analyzes the origins of the rebellion and the repression in greater detail, "Politics, Peasants, and People of Color: The 1912 'Race War' Reconsidered," *Hispanic American Historical Review* 66:3 (1986). Current Cuban perspectives on the war are reflected in the works of Jorge Ibarra, *Cuba: 1898–1921: Partidos políticos y clases sociales* (1992) and the two volume collection published by the Grupo de Estudios Cubanos, *La república neocolonial* (1975–79).

On the social and cultural movements of the 1920s see Louis A. Pérez, Jr., *On Becoming Cuban: Identity, Nationality, and Culture* (1999). Alejandro de la Fuente investigates the politics of race relations in twentieth-century Cuba in *A Nation for All: Race, Inequality, and Politics in Twentieth Century Cuba* (2001). Robin Moore covers the development of Cuban music and other artistic trends in *Nationalizing Blackness: Afrocubanismo and Artistic Revolution in Havana, 1920–1940* (1997). The university student movement is examined in Jaime Suchlicki, *University Students and Revolution in Cuba, 1920–1968* (1969). The history of the labor movement is told by Robert Whitney, *State and Revolution in Cuba: Mass Mobilization and Political Change, 1920–1940* (2001). For pictorial histories of Havana, see Xavier Galmiche, *Havana: Districts of Light* (2001), and Llilian Llanes, *Havana, Then and Now* (2004).

The history of the Machado regime and the events leading to the revolution of 1933 are covered in a number of excellent works, including Luis Aguilar, *Cuba 1933: Prologue to Revolution* (1972) and the memoir by Justo Carillo, *Cuba 1933: Students, Yankees, and Soldiers* (1994). As usual, contemporary Cuban perspectives should not be neglected. For more detail on these events see José A. Tabares de Real, *La revolución del 30: sus dos últimos años* (1973) and Jorge Ibarra, *La mediación del 33: ocaso del machadato* (1999).

CHAPTER FOUR:
THE SECOND REPUBLIC, 1934–1958

The literature on the period prior to 1959 tends to focus on the revolutionary movements of the 1950s. More work remains to be done on all topics from the revolution of 1933 to Batista's coup of 1952, but there are many valuable contributions in addition to the general histories and biographies listed above. Ruby Hart Philips, a *New York Times* correspondent in Cuba during the Batista years, wrote a valuable political history of the period, *Cuba: Island of Paradox* (1959). Herbert Matthews, the *New York Times* journalist who interviewed Castro in 1957, attempted to explain the general origins of the revolution in *Revolution in Cuba: An Essay in Understanding* (1975). Samuel Farber, *Revolution and Reaction in Cuba, 1933–1960* (1976), examines the revolutionary politics of these years from a sociological perspective. For a political history of the Grau and Prio administrations see Charles D. Ameringer, *The Cuban Democratic Experience: The Auténtico Years, 1944–1952* (2000). Louis A. Pérez, Jr., covers the military and political history of the period in *Army Politics in Cuba, 1898–1958* (1976). For a brief overview of the period, see the relevant chapters in Ramon Eduardo Ruíz, *Cuba: The Making of a Revolution* (1968). Irwin Gellman, *Roosevelt and Batista: Good Neighbor Diplomacy in Cuba, 1933–1945* (1973), is an excellent political and diplomatic history of the era.

For a general social and economic history of the period, see Jorge Ibarra, *Prologue to Revolution: Cuba, 1898–1958* (1998). Harold Sims assesses the controversial labor movement in "Cuban Labor and the Communist Party,

1937–1958: An Interpretation," *Cuban Studies* XV (Winter 1985); and also "Collapse of the House of Labor: Ideological Divisions in the Cuban Labor Movement and the U.S. Role, 1944–1949," *Cuban Studies* XXI (1991). Jean Stubbs examines the cigar workers' unions in *Tobacco in the Periphery: A Case Study in Cuban Labour History, 1860–1958* (1985). Maurice Zeitlin, *Revolutionary Politics and the Cuban Working Class* (1967), is based on oral history interviews with Cuban workers. Lowry Nelson, *Rural Cuba* (1950), is a classic study of the Cuban countryside. Julio LeRiverend, *Economic History of Cuba* (1967), is the standard on the subject. Roberto González Echevarría takes us beyond the political turmoil of the period in his superb study of Cuba's favorite pastime in *The Pride of Havana: A History of Cuban Baseball* (1999).

The literature on the insurrection is enormous, and it includes many valuable memoirs and accounts by leading participants. For a general overview see Ramón Bonachea and Marta San Martín, *The Cuban Insurrection, 1952–1959* (1974). Robert Taber, *M-26: Biography of a Revolution* (1961), is a journalistic account by a reporter who interviewed Castro during the insurrection. An entertaining narrative of the revolution focusing on the fall of Batista is provided by John Dorschner and Roberto Fabricio, *The Winds of December: The Cuban Revolution 1958* (1980). Paul Dosal, *Comandante Che: Guerrilla Soldier, Commander, and Strategist, 1956–1967* (2003) tells the story of the insurrection with a special focus on Castro's leading field commander. For a valuable look at the internal workings of the revolutionary movement see Julia Sweig, *Inside the Cuban Revolution: Fidel Castro and the Urban Underground* (2002). A study of the rebellion in Matanzas is provided by Gladys Marel Garcia-Pérez, *Insurrection & Revolution: Armed Struggle in Cuba, 1952–1959* (1998). On the critical topic of United States relations with Cuba during the Batista years, see Jules Robert Benjamin, *The United States and the Origins of the Cuban Revolution: An Empire of Liberty in an Age of National Liberation* (1990); and Thomas Paterson, *Contesting Castro: The United States and the Triumph of the Cuban Revolution* (1994).

The history of the insurrection can also be studied in the lives and writings of its participants. To examine the speeches and writings of Fidel Castro see *Revolutionary Struggle, 1947–1958,* edited by Rolando Bonachea and Nelson Valdés (1972). In addition to the biographies by Robert Quirk and Tad Szulc, see also Georgie Ann Geyer, *Guerrilla Prince: The Untold Story of Fidel Castro* (1991). *Ernesto Che Guevara, Episodes of the Cuban Revolutionary War, 1956–58* (1996), is a history of the rebellion based on the diary Che kept during the war. In *Guerrilla Warfare* (1960), Guevara explains the lessons of the Cuban revolution and the basic strategies of a guerrilla campaign. Several recent biographies of Che Guevara have contributed significantly to our understanding of Cuban history. See Jon Lee Anderson, *Che Guevara: A Revolutionary Life* (1997), and Jorge Castañeda, *Compañero: The Life and Death of Che Guevara* (1997). Carlos Franqui, *Diary of the Cuban Revolution* (1980), is a collection of documents and testimonies compiled by a leading member of the movement. Jane McManus edited and translated a collection of testimonies from lesser-known M-26-7 leaders including Haydée Santamaría and Vílma Espín, *From the Palm Tree: Voices of the Cuban Revolution* (1983). For other accounts by those who struggled against Batista see Enrique Oltuski, *Vida Clandestina: My Life in the Cuban Revolution* (2002); William Gálvez, *1958, invasión rebelde: Camilo y Che* (1998); and Armando Hart Dávalos, *Aldabonazo* (1998). Fulgencio Batista's memoirs, *Cuba Betrayed* (1962), provides insights into the perspective of the Cuban strongman. Earl Smith, U.S. ambassador to Cuba during the Batista years, criticizes American policy in *The Fourth Floor: An Account of the Castro Communist Revolution* (1962). For the perspective of Batista opponents who later broke with Castro see Carlos Franqui, *Family Portrait with Fidel: A Memoir* (1984); Mario Llerena, *The Unsuspected Revolution, The Birth and Rise of Castroism* (1978); and Rufo López Fresquet, *My Fourteen Months with Castro* (1966); and Manuel Urrutia Lleo, *Fidel Castro & Company, Inc.* (1964).

CHAPTER FIVE:
THE REVOLUTION, 1959–1970

The literature on the revolution is enormous, with many of the works focused on the person of Fidel Castro, the Bay of Pigs, and the Missile Crisis. A good starting point is the bibliography edited by Ronald Chilcote, *Cuba, 1953–1978: A Bibliographical Guide to the Literature* (1986). *Cuban Studies/Estudios Cubanos*, an annual journal of the University of Pittsburgh, publishes an up-to-date guide to the literature on Cuba.

The political conflicts of the early years are reflected in the polemical literature written by supporters and opponents of the Revolution, most of it focused on Fidel Castro. The early defenders of Castro and the revolution included North American Marxists Leo Huberman and Paul Sweezy, *Cuba, Anatomy of a Revolution* (1961), French philosopher Jean Paul Sartre, *Sartre on Cuba* (1961), and American journalist Herbert Matthews, *The Cuban Story* (1961). Of the many opponents see Nathaniel Weyl, *Red Star over Cuba* (1972),

Daniel James, *Cuba, the First Soviet Satellite in the Americas* (1961) and Teresa Casuso, *Cuba and Castro* (1964).

For more detached analyses of the political conflicts of the early years see Andrés Suárez, *Cuba: Castroism and Communism* (1967); and K. S. Karol, *Guerrillas in Power: The Course of the Cuban Revolution* (1970). Maurice Halperin probes the course of the Revolution from 1959 to 1968 in two works, *The Rise and Decline of Fidel Castro* (1972) and *The Taming of Fidel Castro* (1981). Two books by Theodore Draper also examine the early years of the Revolution, *Castro's Revolution: Myths and Realities* (1962), and *Castroism: Theory and Practice* (1965).

Much of the debate about the radicalization of the revolution concerns U.S. policy toward Cuba. The literature on the subject includes many valuable scholarly works, though they tend to focus on the Bay of Pigs and the Missile Crisis, with less attention given to the Cuban side of these events. A good place to start is Richard Welch, *Response to Revolution: The United States and the Cuban Revolution, 1959–1961* (1985). Former ambassador Philip Bonsal contributed his perspective on the subject in *Cuba, Castro, and the United States* (1971). Lynn Darrell Bender investigates United States relations with Cuba after 1961, see *The Politics of Hostility: Castro's Revolution and U.S. Policy* (1975). Peter Wyden, *Bay of Pigs: The Untold Story* (1979) is a well-researched narrative written from an American perspective. Grayston Lynch, *Decision for Disaster: The Bay of Pigs* (2003) is a highly critical account of American policy by an American intelligence agent who planned the operation. Victor Andres Triay, *Bay of Pigs: An Oral History of Brigade 2506* (2001), is a sympathetic account of the Cuban exiles who volunteered for the invasion force. For the perspective of the Cuban revolutionaries, the standard account is the four-volume work compiled by Lisandro Otero, *Playa Girón, derrota del imperialismo* (1961–62). Given the polemical nature of the work, students are well advised to go to the primary sources on the subject, especially the collection of declassified U.S. government documents compiled by Luis Aguilar, *Operation Zapata: The "Ultrasensitive" Report and Testimony of the Board of Inquiry on the Bay of Pigs* (1981). See also Peter Kornbluh, ed., *Bay of Pigs Declassified: The Secret CIA Report on the Invasion of Cuba* (1998).

The literature on the Missile Crisis has been strengthened thanks to the information coming out of two conferences involving leaders of Cuba, the United States, and the Soviet Union. For the testimony of the participants see the volumes edited by James Blight, Bruce Allyn, and David Welch, *Back to the Brink: Proceedings of the Moscow Conference on the Cuban Missile Crisis, January 27–28, 1989* (1992); and *Cuba on the Brink: Castro, the Missile Crisis, and the Soviet Collapse* (1993). Aleksandr Fursenko and Timothy J. Naftali, *One Hell of a Gamble: Khrushchev, Castro, and Kennedy, 1958–1964* (1998) utilize declassified Soviet documents to analyze Soviet and American perspectives simultaneously. With the exceptions of Castro's testimony in the conferences, Cuban perceptions of the crisis are generally ignored.

On the restructuring of Cuba in the 1960s see Richard Fagen, *The Transformation of Political Culture in Cuba* (1969), which includes a study of the literacy campaign. Leo Huberman and Paul Sweezy offer a sympathetic account of the social and economic reforms in *Socialism in Cuba* (1969). Economist Carmelo Mesa-Lago analyzes policies and performance in *The Economy of Socialist Cuba: A Two-Decade Appraisal* (1981). René Dumont, an advisor to the Cuban government, provides a critical assessment of the agricultural sector in *Cuba: Socialism and Development* (1970). Collections of interviews, speeches, and writings are also important for the study of these years. James Petras edited a collection of major speeches, *Fidel Castro Speaks* (1969). For a rare glimpse into the life of the Cuba's controversial leader see Lee Lockwood, *Castro's Cuba, Cuba's Fidel* (1969), a valuable collection of extensive interviews and photographs of Castro in the late 1960s. The writings and speeches of Che Guevara also provide insight into policy and performance in the 1960s, see Rolando E. Bonachea and Nelson P. Valdéz, eds., *Che: Selected Works of Ernesto Guevara* (1969). Mary-Alice Waters edited *The Bolivian Diary of Ernesto Che Guevara* (1994), the primary source for accounts of Guevara's ill-fated campaign. Felix Rodríguez, a Cuban-born CIA agent who tracked Che down in Bolivia recounts his experience in *Shadow Warrior: The CIA Hero of a Hundred Unknown Battles* (1989). Cuba's efforts to foment revolution throughout Latin America are examined in William Ratliff, *Castroism and Communism in Latin America, 1959–1976: The Varieties of Marxist-Leninist Experience* (1976).

CHAPTER SIX:
THE LAST REVOLUTIONARY, 1970–2005

In addition to the general work on the revolution by Marifeli Perez-Stable, Juan M. del Aguila, *Cuba, Dilemmas of a Revolution,* 3d ed. (1994), and Max Azicri, *Cuba Today and Tomorrow: Reinventing Socialism* (2000), focus on the period since 1959. The eleven different editions of Irving Louis Horowitz and Jaime Suchlicki, eds., *Cuban Communism, 1959–2003,* 11th ed. (2003), contain articles on a wide range of topics by a variety of Cuban experts. A recent biography by former British ambassador Leycester Coltman, *The Real Fidel Castro* (2003), updates the previous biographies by Szulc, Quirk, and Georgie Ann Geyer.

For a detailed analysis of the institutionalization of the revolution in the 1970s, see Jorge Domínguez, *Cuba: Order and Revolution* (1978). Carmelo Mesa-Lago investigates economic and social changes in *Cuba in the 1970s: Pragmatism and Institutionalization* (1974). Jacques Levesque analyzes Soviet-Cuban relations in *The USSR and the Cuban Revolution: Soviet Ideological and Strategical Perspectives, 1959–77* (1978). Andrew Zimbalist and Claes Brundenius extend the analysis into the 1980s in *The Cuban Economy: Measurement and Analysis of Socialist Performance* (1989). On United States relations with Cuba during the 1970s, see the account by American diplomat Wayne Smith, *The Closest of Enemies: A Personal and Diplomatic Account of U.S.-Cuban Relations since 1957* (1987). For a general study of Cuba's foreign policy see Jorge Dominguez, *To Make a World Safe for Revolution* (1989).

For a personal account of the revolution see Oscar Lewis, Ruth Lewis, and Susan Rigdon, *Four Men—Living the Revolution: An Oral History of Contemporary Cuba* (1977). On race relations in revolutionary Cuba see Pedro Pérez Sarduy and Jean Stubbs, eds., *AfroCuba: An Anthology of Cuban Writings on Race, Politics, and Culture* (1993). For a critical perspective by a Cuban exile see Carlos Moore, *Castro, the Blacks, and Africa* (1988). Yvonne Daniel, *Rumba: Dance and Social Change in Contemporary Cuba* (1995), examines Cuban dance culture in the revolutionary period. Katherine J. Hagedorn explores Afro-Cuban religions in *Divine Utterances: The Performance of Afro-Cuban Santería* (2001). For a complete survey of athletic competition, see Paula J. Pettavino and Geralyn Pye, *Sport in Cuba: The Diamond in the Rough* (1994).

On Cuban women see the insightful accounts compiled by Margaret Randall, *Cuban Women Now: Interviews with Cuban Women* (1974), and Oscar Lewis, Ruth Lewis, and Susan Rigdon, *Four Women—Living the Revolution: An Oral History of Contemporary Cuba* (1977). For primary sources on the subject, including speeches by Vílma Espín, see Elizabeth Stone, ed., *Women and the Cuban Revolution* (1981). Lynn Stoner examines the prerevolutionary history of women in *From the House to the Streets: The Cuban Woman's Movement for Legal Reform, 1898–1940* (1991).

To understand the history and perspective of the Cubans who fled the revolution see Maria Cristina García, *Havana USA: Cuban Exiles and Cuban Americans in South Florida, 1959–1994* (1997). On the persecution of dissidents in Cuba see Armando Valladares, *Against All Hope: A Memoir of Life in Castro's Gulag* (1986). Novelist Reinaldo Arenas describes his persecution for being a dissident writer and homosexual in *Before Night Falls* (1993).

A controversial starting point for a study of the Special Period is the journalistic account of Andres Oppenheimer, *Castro's Final Hour: The Secret Story behind the Coming Downfall of Communist Cuba* (1992). Carollee Bengelsdorf, *The Problem of Democracy in Cuba: Between Vision and Reality* (1994), provides an academic examination of Cuba's response to the collapse of its socialist allies in Eastern Europe. See also the collection of essays edited by Carmelo Mesa-Lago, *Cuba after the Cold War* (1993). For a general overview of Cuban-Soviet relations, see Yuri Pavlov, *Soviet-Cuban Alliance, 1959–1991* (1994). For critiques of American policy toward Cuba see Donna Rich Kaplowitz, *Anatomy of a Failed Embargo: U.S. Sanctions Against Cuba* (1998); and Peter Schwab, *Cuba: Confronting the U.S. Embargo* (1998). For a more balanced analysis of American policy see Morris Morley and Chris McGillion, *Unfinished Business: America and Cuba after the Cold War, 1989–2001* (2002). Mark Falcoff provides a sober analysis and critique of American policy in *Cuba: The Morning After: Confronting Castro's Legacy* (2003).

Several scholars attempt to explain how ordinary Cubans survive during a time of deep economic crisis. See Ben Corbett, *This is Cuba: An Outlaw Culture Survives* (2002); Catherine Moses, *Real Life in Castro's Cuba* (1999); and Ana Julia Jata-Hausmann, *The Cuban Way: Capitalism, Communism, and Confrontation* (1999). Juan Lopez attempts to explain the failure of Cuba to liberalize in *Democracy Delayed: The Case of Castro's Cuba* (2002). Damian Fernandez analyzes political culture and the transition to civil society in *Cuba and the Politics of Passion* (2000).

❧ Index ❧

Keith, Minor, 49
Kennedy, John F.: Cuban missile crisis and, 96–97; plans to overthrow Castro, 91–93, 95
Keppel, George (Lord of Albemarle), 12–13
Khrushchev, Nikita, 90, 96–97
King Ranch (Texas), 70
Korean War, 69

labor organizing and unions: in anti-Machado movement, 59–60; governmental co-opting of, 73; governmental reforms and, 60–61; in post-WWI depression, 52–53. See also working classes
Lam, Wilfredo, 75
Lansky, Meyer, 71, 72
La Plata: battle of, 78
Laredu Bru, Federico, 57
Latin America: support for liberation movements in, 95, 101–3, 110–11
Liberal party, 45, 46, 47
literacy campaign, 93–94, 113, 118
literature, 75–76, 100–101
Lodge, Henry Cabot, 39
López, Narciso, 29
lottery profits, 46–47

Maceo, Gen. Antonio ("Bronze Titan"): background of, 24; claims to legacy of, 77; death of, 38; goals of, 32–33, 35; in PRC uprising, 31, 33–34, 36, 37–38
Maceo, Marcos, 24
Machado, Gerardo, 54, 57–60
Macuriges (Cuba): slave rebellions in, 25
Magoon, Charles, 46
Mañach, Jorge, 54–55
Marianao (Cuba): music in, 54; Orfila shootout in, 66–67
Marianao Tigers (baseball team), 75
Mariel boatlift, 111, 114
Martí, José: background of, 35; claims to legacy of, 63, 66, 76, 77; death of, 2–3; education about, 110; invasion plan of, 37; on U.S., 41; vision of, 1–3, 24, 35–36, 46, 47, 52, 93, 125

Martínez Campos, Gen. Arsenio, 33, 38
Martínez Saenz, Joaquín, 59
Martínez Villena, Rubén, 55
Marx, Karl, 93, 98, 110
Masferrer, Rolando, 66, 68
Masó, Bartolomé, 44
Matanzas (Cuba): slave rebellions in, 25; slaves on plantations near, 26
Matos, Huber, 88
Matthews, Herbert, 78
Máximo Líder, 85. See also Castro, Fidel
McKinley, William, 39–40, 42–44
media coverage: of Castro's insurrection, 78; of Castro's triumphal procession and speech, 83–84; of Castro's U.S. visit, 87; censorship and, 100–101, 110; of Maine explosion, 39; of Weyler's concentration camps, 38–39
Mella, Julio Antonio, 55, 57–59
Mendieta, Carlos, 57, 61
Menocal, Mario, 47, 48, 61
mercantilism, 9–10, 11–12
Mesa-Lago, Carmelo, 100
Mexico: liberation movements in, 18
Mikoyan, Anastas, 88
military force (Castro's): barbudos in, 81, 82; corruption in, 120–21; guerrilla warfare and, 77–81, 102–3; INRA and, 87–88; purging of, 85–86; training of, 76; U.S. planes shot down by, 123; U.S. plans to overthrow Castro and, 91–93; women in, 116–18. See also civilian militias
military force (Spanish): Cubans in, 21–22; planters protected by, 15, 17, 19; PRC rebellion and, 36–38, 39; rebellion crushed in 1877, 33; U.S. army's defeat of, 40–41
Minoristas (group), 55
Miñoso, Orestes "Minnie," 75
Miró Cardona, José, 85
Monroe, James, 21, 40
Monroe Doctrine (1823), 21
Montejo, Esteban, 56
Moore, Robin, 54
Morales, Nicolás, 17

people of color: athletic opportunities for, 115–16; benefits of revolution for, 112–16; hotels' discrimination against, 122–23; political party of, 47, 48, 112; as refugees, 111, 114. *See also* African Cubans; race relations

People's Republic of China: Cuban sugar for, 90

Perez, Faustino, 85

Pérez, Louis: on corruption, 65, 72; on sugar industry, 69; on suicide, 127; on television stereotypes, 74; on women's roles, 118

Pérez Prado, Dámaso, 74

Pérez San Román, Lt. Dionisio, 79

Philippines: U.S. control of, 43

Phinney, Theodore, 26

Picasso, Pablo, 75

PIC (*Partido Independiente de Color*, Independent Party of Color), 47, 48, 112

Pierce, Franklin, 29

pirates, 10

Plácido (Gabriel de la Concepción Valdés), 26–27

planters: annexationist movement and, 19–20, 28–29; *colonos* as (small), 50, 70; eastern/western divisions in, 27–28, 31; fears of, 15–18, 32; profits from triangular trade, 14, 24–30; punishments used by, 25–27; Spanish military's protection of, 15, 17, 19; U.S. companies' displacement of, 34–35. *See also* sugar industry; tobacco industry

Platt, Orville H., 43

Platt Amendment (1901): criticism of, 55; Cuban repeal of, 60, 61–62; effects of, 45–46, 48; irrelevance of, 56; passage of, 43–44. *See also* Reciprocity Treaty (1903)

police force: gang influence in, 66; repression by, 54, 58, 109–10. *See also* military force (Castro's)

politics: Cuban identity in, 53–56; in First Republic, 45–48; gangsterism in, 66–67; martyrdom in, 127; in Second Republic, 64–67

Polk, James, 29

poor people: Castro supported by, 93; health care for, 109; illiteracy of, 93; revolutionary hopes of, 88–89; rural conditions for, 73, 110

PPC. *See Partido del Pueblo Cubano* (PPC, Cuban People's Party, Ortodoxos)

PRC. *See* Cuban Revolutionary Party (PRC)

PRC-A. *See Partido Revolucionario Cubano-Auténtico* (PRC-A, Cuban Revolutionary Party, Auténticos)

Preston, Andrew, 49

Prío Socarrás, Carlos, 63, 65–67, 77, 85

prostitution, 122–23

Protest of Baraguá, 33

Protest of the Thirteen, 55

PSP (*Partido Socialista Popular*, Popular Socialist Party), 86, 87–88

Puerto Príncipe (Cuba): founding of, 6; slave rebellions in, 25

Puerto Rico: liberation movement and, 21; U.S. control of, 43

Quesada, Gen. Manuel, 31

race relations: in pre-revolutionary Cuba, 35–36, 111–12; recent tourism and, 123; in revolutionary Cuba, 112–16

railway system, 50

ranching industry, 70, 87–88

Real Compañia de Comercio, 12

Recio de Oquendo, Gonzalo, 13

Reciprocity Treaty (1903): economic effects of, 69–70; function of, 48–49, 51; irrelevance of, 56

reconcentration policy (Weyler's), 38–39

Reform party (Cuban), 30

Revolución (newspaper), 85

Revolution: austerity period in, 121–24; consolidation of, 84, 85–87; defense of, 95–97; definition of, 88–93; failure of, 125–26; institutionalization of, 106–11; nationalization in, 87, 89–90, 98, 99, 123; people of color and, 112–16; promise to spread, 95, 101–3; radicalization of, 87–89; rectification (purge) campaign in, 120–21; refugees

from, 90–91, 93; spirit and dedication in, 98–104; triumph of, 83–84; U.S. plans to overthrow, 88, 91–93, 95; women in, 116–20
rice plantations, 87
Rickover, Adm. Hyman, 40
Rodríguez, Carlos Rafael, 99
Rogers, Ginger, 71
Roosevelt, Franklin D., 59, 61
Roosevelt, Theodore, 39, 40–42, 44–45
Ruíz, Fabio, 66
Ruíz, Ramon Eduardo, 65
rumba, 115
rural areas: eastern/western divisions in, 27–28, 31, 47; improvements hampered in, 110; literacy brigades in, 94; medical services in, 109; people of color in, 112; revolutionaries in, 102; tourism in, 73

Salabarría, Mario, 66, 67
salsa music, 54, 74
Sánchez Arango, Aureliano, 63
Sánchez Manduley, Celia, 77–78, 116–17
Sánchez Mosquera (lieutenant), 78
Sancti Spiritus (Cuba): founding of, 6
Sanguily, Gen. Manuel, 57
San Martín, José de, 18
San Román, Lt. Pepé, 93
Sans Souci (club), 71, 72
Santa Clara (Cuba): Castro's insurrection and, 81; slaves on plantations near, 26
Santa Coloma, Boris Luís, 116
Santamaría, Abel, 68, 116
Santamaría, Haydée, 116–17
Santería religion, 115
Santiago (Cuba): British attack on, 10; Castro's insurrection and, 68, 82; founding of, 6; País's attack on, 77; U.S. Marines in, 48
Santo Domingo: white settlers from, 27
Second Declaration of Havana, 113
Second Republic (1934–1958): Batista's control of, 64–72; Castro's insurrection against, 76–82; demolition of, 85; denunciations of, 63–64; nationalism and

Americanization in, 72–76; politics of, 64–67
self-employment, 107, 121
Septeto Habanero (group), 54
Seven Years War (1755–63), 12
sexuality, 119–20
Shafter, Gen. William R., 43
Shell Oil Company, 89
slaves and slavery: annexationist movement and, 28–29, 31–32; conditions for, 24; culture retained by, 19; gradual abolition of, 30, 35; persistence in Cuba, 25, 28; rebellions of, 15–18, 20–21, 25, 26; rebels' desire to free, 32–34
slave trade: in 1856–60, 29–30; abolished, 18–19, 35; British control of, 11, 13; sugar production and, 14–15; in triangular trade with sugar, 14, 24–30
small businesses, 107, 121
socialism: of Castro vs. Gorbachev, 105–6; debates on how to implement, 98–99; as liberating individuals, 100; realities juxtaposed to, 106–7
son (music and dance form), 53–54
Sonora Matancera (group), 54, 74
Sores, Jacques, 7
Sorí Marín, Humberto, 87
South Africa: apartheid in, 113
South Sea Company (British), 11
sovereignty, 43–44, 54–55. See also independence
Soviet Union. See Union of Soviet Socialist Republics (USSR)
Spain: colonialism of, 8–10, 13, 31; conquest by, 5–8; convoy system of, 7–8; Cuban crisis and, 39; Cuban rebellion against, 23–24; Cuban representation in, 15, 28, 30; declining power of, 11, 12, 14, 21–22; economic society chartered by, 15; exploration by, 4; French occupation of, 18; Glorious Revolution in, 23; Havana surrendered by, 13; Martí's exile in, 35; mercantilism of, 9–10, 11–12; reformist movement suppressed by, 30–31; slave liberation threatened by, 28; slave trade abolished by, 18–19; treasure

Cuba Libre: A Brief History of Cuba
Developmental editor and copy editor: Andrew J. Davidson
Production editor: Lucy Herz
Proofreader: Claudia Siler
Cartographers: Jane Domier, Jason Casanova
Indexer: Margie Towery
Cover Designer: Christopher Calvetti, c2itgraphics
Printer: Versa Press, Inc.